I0901228

Among the titles in this series

EDITED AND INTRODUCED BY MARY-ALICE WATERS

Cuba and the Independence War in Guinea-Bissau and Cape Verde: The Fall of the Last Colonial Empire in Africa
VÍCTOR DREKE (2025)

Revolution and the Road to Peace in Colombia
FIDEL CASTRO (2025, 2023)

Che Guevara on Economics and Politics in the Transition to Socialism
CARLOS TABLADA (2024, 1998)

Our History Is Still Being Written
ARMANDO CHOY, GUSTAVO CHUI, AND MOISÉS SÍO WONG (2017, 2005)

Cuba and Angola: The War for Freedom
HARRY VILLEGAS (2017)

"It's the Poor Who Face the Savagery of the US 'Justice' System"
THE CUBAN FIVE TALK ABOUT THEIR LIVES
WITHIN THE US WORKING CLASS (2016)

Women in Cuba: The Making of a Revolution Within the Revolution
VILMA ESPÍN, ASELA DE LOS SANTOS, AND YOLANDA FERRER (2012)

Capitalism and the Transformation of Africa
MARY-ALICE WATERS, MARTÍN KOPPEL (2009)

Cuba and the Coming American Revolution
JACK BARNES (2007)

The First and Second Declarations of Havana
(2007)

Playa Girón/Bay of Pigs
FIDEL CASTRO AND JOSÉ RAMÓN FERNÁNDEZ (2001)

Che Guevara Talks to Young People
(2000)

Making History
INTERVIEWS WITH FOUR CUBAN GENERALS (1999)

How Far We Slaves Have Come!
NELSON MANDELA AND FIDEL CASTRO (1991)

MARIANAS IN COMBAT

MARIANAS IN COMBAT

Teté Puebla & the Mariana Grajales Women's Platoon in Cuba's revolutionary war 1956–58

PATHFINDER

New York · London · Montreal · Sydney

Edited by Mary-Alice Waters

ISBN 978-0-87348-957-7
Library of Congress Control Number 2002115680
Manufactured in Canada

First edition, 2003
Thirteenth printing, 2026

COVER AND PHOTO PAGES DESIGN: Eva Braiman
COVER PHOTO: Members of the Mariana Grajales Women's Platoon and other female Rebel Army combatants, January 1959. Teté Puebla is standing, at center. (Courtesy Teté Puebla)

Pathfinder
pathfinderpress.com
Email: pathfinder@pathfinderpress.com

Contents

Foreword

HAVANA, NOVEMBER 19, 2002
Year of the Heroes Imprisoned by the Empire

After reading the valuable book based on the interview with our comrade in struggle, Brigadier General Delsa Esther "Teté" Puebla Viltres, I believe it's best not to add words by way of a preface, but rather to let Teté's straightforward answers help readers discover for themselves her humanism, her humble origin, her revolutionary fiber, and to appreciate more deeply the generosity and firmness of our revolution.

She says she has lived the revolution so intensely that she cannot separate it from her life. We might add that through her account the reader will learn to admire Teté and have a better understanding of the justice of our cause.

Juan Almeida Bosque
President
Association of Combatants of the Cuban Revolution

GRANMA

Brig. Gen. Teté Puebla receiving Heroine of the Republic of Cuba decoration from Fidel Castro, December 2, 2001. Vilma Espín, who received the same distinction, is looking on.

Teté Puebla

DELSA ESTHER "TETÉ" PUEBLA, a brigadier general in Cuba's Revolutionary Armed Forces, was a combatant in the 1956–58 revolutionary war and a founding member of the Communist Party of Cuba and Federation of Cuban Women (FMC). She was born December 9, 1940, in the town of Yara in eastern Cuba.

In 1956, during her first year at the Teacher Training School in Manzanillo, she joined the underground July 26 Movement, which was fighting to bring down the U.S.-backed tyranny of Fulgencio Batista. She took numerous tasks and assignments over the next year, until a member of the movement was arrested and talked under torture, telling of Puebla's involvement. She left her studies in July 1957 and went to the Sierra Maestra mountains, where she became a member of the Rebel Army.

In September 1958 she became a founding member and second in command of the Mariana Grajales Women's Platoon, the first female combat unit of the Rebel Army. As a lieutenant, she took part in numerous battles between September and the revolution's victory in January 1959. Since then her responsibilities have included:

- From February 1959, director of the Rebel Army's Department of Assistance to War Victims and their families.

- From February 1963, head of education in the Eastern Army.
- From August 1964, in charge of the Children's Farms for war orphans and of Social Security within the Western Army.
- From April 1966, working in a Special Unit to attend to the family members of internationalist volunteers.
- From March 1969, director of the Guaicanamar Cattle Plan in Jaruco, in Havana province.
- From October 1978, head of the military section of the Communist Party in Havana.

From 1985 until the present, Teté Puebla has served as director of the office responsible for Assistance to Combatants and Family Members of Internationalists and Martyrs of the Revolution.

A member of the Revolutionary Armed Forces for forty-six years, she attained the rank of lieutenant in 1958, captain in 1959, and colonel in 1994. In 1996 she was promoted to brigadier general.

From 1980 to 1986 she was a member of the Central Committee of the Communist Party of Cuba. From 1980 until the present she has been a member of the party's Provincial Committee in Havana and its Ideological Commission.

She is a deputy to Cuba's National Assembly, representing Central Havana municipality, and is a member of the assembly's Permanent Defense Commission.

She has been a member of the Federation of Cuban Women (FMC) since 1960. From 1980 to 1989 she served on its National Committee, and is currently a member of its City of Havana provincial committee.

She serves on the National Executive of the Association of Combatants of the Cuban Revolution (ACRC), as well as the provincial executive committee.

Since 1960 she has been married to Raúl Castro Mercader, who she met as a Rebel Army officer in Che Guevara's column in the revolutionary war. He is today a brigadier general in the Revolutionary Armed Forces. They have three children and five grandchildren.

In December 2001 Teté Puebla received the title Hero of the Republic of Cuba, the country's highest honor.

LUIS MADRID / MILITANT

Brigadier General Teté Puebla (right) and editor Mary-Alice Waters, Havana, November 18, 2000.

Mary-Alice Waters, the author of the introduction and editor of *Marianas in Combat,* is president of Pathfinder Press and editor of the Marxist magazine *New International.* She joined the socialist movement in the United States in the early 1960s under the impact of the expanding mass struggle for Black rights and the victories being won by Cuba's working people as they defended their socialist revolution against Washington's assaults. She has been a member of the National Committee of the Socialist Workers Party since 1967.

Waters is the author, among other titles, of *Feminism and the Marxist Movement* and "Defending Cuba, Defending Cuba's Socialist Revolution." She is the editor of *Rosa Luxemburg Speaks,* of *Cosmetics, Fashions, and the Exploitation of Women,* and nearly a dozen books of interviews, speeches and writings by leaders of the Cuban Revolution.

Introduction

Before the revolutionary victory, women were objects—mere bed decorations. After the revolution this changed. Women began to organize massively, working to change the conditions of their lives and to free themselves.

TETÉ PUEBLA
Marianas in Combat

The change in a historical epoch can always be determined by the progress of women toward freedom. . . . The degree of emancipation of woman is the natural measure of general emancipation.

KARL MARX
The Holy Family

Brigadier General Teté Puebla, the highest-ranking woman in Cuba's Revolutionary Armed Forces and a Hero of the Cuban Revolution, joined the struggle to overthrow the bloody U.S.-backed dictatorship of Fulgencio Batista in 1956, when she was fifteen years old. *Marianas in Combat* is her story—from clandestine action in the small town of Yara in the foothills of eastern Cuba's Sierra Maestra mountains, to officer in the Rebel Army's first all-women's platoon, to protagonist in and defender of the social and economic transformation of Cuba.

On January 1, 1959, barely two years after the initiation of the revolutionary war, Batista's army disintegrated in face of the rapidly advancing forces of the Rebel Army and the spreading popular insurrection and general strike called by the July 26 Movement. The dictator and his closest entourage of murderers and thieves fled Cuba. What millions of Cubans came to proudly call "The First Free Territory of the Americas" was born.

The new revolutionary power, responding to spreading mobilizations of working people, set out to change the living and working conditions of millions of ordinary Cubans. In doing so they ignored the supposedly inherent prerogatives of wealthy U.S. families and their retainers in Cuba who decades earlier had taken control of the island nation's lucrative sugar plantations, cattle ranches, nickel reserves, oil refineries, railroads, utilities monopolies, and banks.

Within a few months' time, the first elements of a more equitable social order had been established. A sweeping land reform program had recognized the title of 100,000 peasant families to the land they had been working. Onerous rents, telephone charges, electricity rates, and other utility fees had been slashed. Public education and health care had been expanded to all social layers in Cuba. Racial discrimination in employment and public activities had been outlawed. The brothels and casinos built for the pleasure and titillation of the imperialist lords and ladies had been closed. And hundreds of thousands of workers and peasants, especially the youth, had poured into the newly created revolutionary militias to arm and train themselves to defend their gains.

As Washington's antagonism to this popular and patriotic course sharpened, Cuban working people and their government refused to back down. The revolution deepened and grew stronger in the face of U.S.-organized and -financed sabotage, subversion, assassination plots, and countless acts of murderous terrorism directed at the population. In April

1961, in less than seventy-two hours of intense combat, a full-scale U.S.-orchestrated mercenary invasion at the Bay of Pigs was crushed by the determined response of the popular militias and revolutionary police and armed forces. The victory at Playa Girón, as the battle is known in Cuba, marked a decisive turning point in the revolution.

From these years of titanic class struggle, the first socialist revolution in the Western Hemisphere emerged.

In the pages that follow we meet some of the ordinary women and men—many, like Teté Puebla, still in their teens at the time—who made this history. We see how they were themselves transformed in the course of the struggle. We begin to understand the class trajectory that for more than forty years has enabled Cuba's working people to hold U.S. imperialism at bay as they defend their course, building a new society based on economic and social relations that are the negation of the dog-eat-dog realities of capitalism.

We see how the door to advances such as those registered by women in Cuba over the last half century can be opened only as working people in their majority act to break the stranglehold of the propertied classes, the beneficiaries of the second-class status of women. And we see why a revolutionary cadre committed to advancing women's equality is decisive to reaching that goal.

■

Some eight years after the triumph over Batista, Cuban Prime Minister Fidel Castro, addressing a plenary meeting of the Federation of Cuban Women in December 1966, drew attention to the number of women who were shouldering weighty and challenging new tasks in agricultural programs where widespread social prejudices would previously have prevented them from assuming leadership responsibilities. Among their ranks, as she describes in these pages, was soon to be Teté Puebla. "This is one of the great lessons," Castro noted,

> one of the greatest victories over prejudices that have existed, not just for decades or centuries, but for millennia. We refer to the prejudice that all a woman was capable of was to scrub dishes, wash and iron clothes, cook, keep house, and bear children [*Applause and shouts*]—an age-old prejudice that placed women in an inferior position in society. In effect, she did not have a productive place in society.
>
> Such prejudices are thousands of years old and have survived through various social systems. If we're talking about capitalism, women—that is, lower-class women—were doubly exploited or doubly humiliated. A poor woman, as a part of the working class or a working-class family, was exploited simply because she was poor, because she was a worker.
>
> But in addition, even though she was herself a worker, within her own class she was scorned and underrated. Not only was she underestimated, exploited, and scorned by the exploiting classes, but even within her own class she was the object of innumerable prejudices. . . .
>
> If women in our country were doubly exploited, doubly humiliated in the past, then this simply means that women in a social revolution should be doubly revolutionary. [*Applause*]
>
> And this perhaps is the explanation, or at least provides the social basis, for the resolute, enthusiastic, firm, and loyal support given by Cuban women to this revolution.
>
> This revolution has really been two revolutions for women; it has meant a double liberation: as part of the

> exploited sectors of the country, and second, as women, who were discriminated against not only as workers but also as women, in that society of exploitation.
>
> The attitude of Cuban women toward the revolution corresponds to this reality; it corresponds to what the revolution has meant to them. . . .
>
> There are two sectors in this country, two components of society that, aside from economic reasons, have had other motives for sympathizing with and feeling enthusiasm for the revolution: the black population of Cuba and the country's women.

Teté Puebla's account provides a vivid and concrete picture of this revolutionary transformation. We see what involvement in the struggle meant for one young woman from a poor family of working people in Oriente province—how and why she refused to accept the status quo, her hopes and achievements, how she grew and changed as the war intensified. In the Rebel Army camps of the Sierras, she relates, "what we wanted more than anything was to earn the right to fight." In words that capture the determined struggle of women everywhere to establish their equality, she notes that "we had already proved that women could do just about everything. . . . 'If women have to take part in all the duties of the revolution,' we said, 'why can't we fight the same way as our men fight?' "

After a major offensive by the troops of the Batista regime had been defeated in July 1958, and as the Rebel Army was preparing to launch the counteroffensive that would carry them to victory, "we asked our commander in chief to allow us to fight arms in hand. He agreed. Fidel said yes, women had won the right to fight with a rifle, face to face with the enemy."

The political battle waged by Fidel Castro and those closest to him within the leadership of the Rebel Army to take on the antiwoman prejudices that were then still deeply ingrained even in some of the best combatants, and to establish the Mariana Grajales Women's Platoon, is a measure of the caliber of that revolutionary leadership. It was one of the most important steps taken by the Rebel Army command in the midst of the war, demonstrating in practice the social course, the class course, that would continue to be followed by the new revolutionary power once victory over the dictatorship had been won.

To the men who complained—"How can we give rifles to women when there are so many men who are unarmed?"—Fidel responded, "Because they're better soldiers than you are. They're more disciplined." The Marianas' record in combat proved that the decision to organize the platoon was right, and their actions helped open the way to further gains for women as the revolution advanced.

The name of the squad could not have been more appropriate. The Rebel Army unit of which Teté Puebla was second in command was named after a heroine of Cuba's wars of independence from Spanish colonial rule in the nineteenth century. Mariana Grajales was a black woman who sent all her sons to fight for Cuba's freedom; eight members of her family were killed in battle. The most prominent was her son the Bronze Titan, Antonio Maceo, the legendary general of Cuba's independence army, killed in battle in 1896. Her name has come to symbolize the spirit of resistance and unbreakable courage of the oppressed fighting for their liberation the world over.

■

The interview printed in these pages took place in Havana, Cuba, in two sessions, the first on November 18, 2000, and the second on March 1, 2002. It was made possible through the support and encouragement of the leadership of the Association of Combatants of the Cuban Revolution, especially its president, Commander of the Revolution Juan Almeida, who authored the foreword to this volume, and Brigadier General Harry Villegas, who is today the executive vice president of the association.

Without the assistance, perseverance, and capacities of Cuban editor Iraida Aguirrechu, it would not have been possible to bring the manuscript to completion with anything close to the quality and accuracy desired and, we hope, realized.

Special appreciation goes to Teté Puebla herself for the time and attention she generously gave, and for the selection of irreplaceable original photos from her personal archives.

Help in assembling the photo pages was also provided by Delfín Xiqués of *Granma* and the leadership of the Federation of Cuban Women, as well as Manuel Martínez of *Bohemia*.

The glossary, annotation, and much of the editorial preparation in English was the work of Pathfinder editor Michael Taber. Pathfinder editor Luis Madrid participated in the first interview with Teté Puebla and was responsible for final preparation of the text in Spanish. Martín Koppel, the editor of *Perspectiva Mundial*, participated in the second interview session.

A large team of volunteers who are part of the international Pathfinder Reprint Project made possible the simultaneous publication of this book in Spanish and English. They made their time and abilities available to translate, copy edit, format, proofread, prepare photos and maps, and competently dispatch many other tasks indispensable to prepare the manuscript for press.

Through the collective efforts of many, one more strand of the rich history of the Cuban Revolution is now accessible to all. *Marianas in Combat* is dedicated to the young people in every corner of the earth who today, like fifteen-year-old Teté Puebla before them, refuse to accept the brutality and injustice of the capitalist system that surrounds them and decide to join with others in a disciplined fight for a better world.

Mary-Alice Waters
November 2002

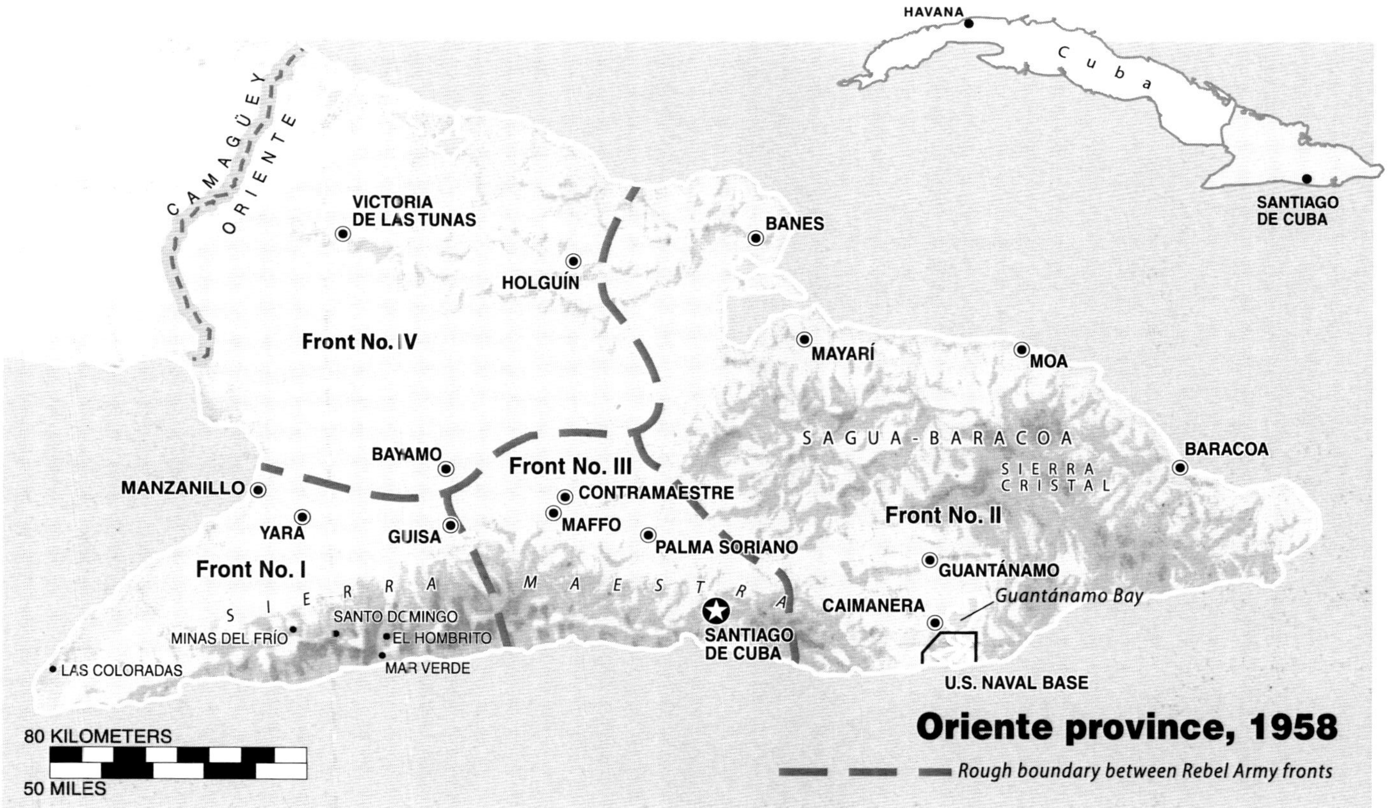

Oriente province, 1958

HAVANA
MATANZAS
JARUCO
HAVANA
MATANZAS
GUANIGUANICO
PINAR DEL RÍO
PINAR DEL RÍO
SANTA CLARA
LAS VILLAS
ESCAMBRAY
PLAYA GIRÓN
Isle of Pines

ATLANTIC OCEAN
GULF OF MEXICO
Bahamas
Puerto Rico
Cuba
Haiti
Jamaica
Dominican Republic
Mexico
Br. Honduras (Belize)
Honduras
Guatemala
El Salvador
CARIBBEAN SEA
Nicaragua
Costa Rica
PACIFIC OCEAN
Panama
Colombia
Venezuela

CAMAGÜEY
CAMAGÜEY
HOLGUÍN
ORIENTE
SAGUA-BARACOA
MANZANILLO
YARA
SIERRA MAESTRA
SANTIAGO DE CUBA
GUANTÁNAMO
U.S. NAVAL BASE
160 KILOMETERS
100 MILES

Cuba 1959

‘I am and will always be a Mariana in combat’

INTERVIEW WITH TETÉ PUEBLA

COURTESY TETÉ PUEBLA

Lieutenant Teté Puebla, second in command of the Mariana Grajales Platoon, in Matanzas, during the Liberty Caravan, January 1959.

From the underground to the Sierra

MARY-ALICE WATERS: One of the best measures of the character of the Cuban Revolution is the profound changes it has brought in the economic, social, and political status of women. All over the world there are revolutionary-minded fighters—men and women both—who support women's equality and are interested in understanding this transformation. How was it accomplished? What kind of leadership made it possible?

For almost five decades you've taken on major responsibilities in the struggle by Cuban working people to defend and deepen their revolution, transforming their country and themselves and affecting the course of history. Today you're a brigadier general in the Revolutionary Armed Forces of Cuba. All this must have been beyond your wildest imagination when you joined the struggle as a teenager. How did a young woman growing up in a small town in Oriente province in the mid-1950s find her way into the revolutionary movement to overthrow the Batista dictatorship?

TETÉ PUEBLA: I'm from a very poor peasant family in the municipality of Yara, in what's today Granma province in eastern Cuba. My father was a peasant who farmed a small plot of land. I'm the oldest of eight sisters and brothers.

I was raised by my grandparents, and when I was growing up I never had any store-bought toys. All I had were rag dolls made by my grandmother. I always dreamed of having a real doll.

I was an active youth. I rode a bicycle, roller-skated. I'd dive from the bridge into the river and swim. I rode horses. I was always dancing the cha cha cha, the mambo. I also played baseball—hard, not the way a little girl was supposed to play. I liked to be the pitcher.

All these things helped prepare me for life, for the war.

My entire family supported or belonged to the July 26 Revolutionary Movement. Two of my brothers later joined the Rebel Army, and all my uncles ended up in the Sierra Maestra as rebel officers. So mine's a guerrilla family, a revolutionary family. Myself, I joined the July 26 Movement when I was fifteen. I was living in Yara and going to school in Manzanillo.

LUIS MADRID: What was the political situation in Cuba at that time?

PUEBLA: It was critical. The Batista dictatorship was carrying out murders and abuses against the people.

There was a special unit of the tyranny at the time called Masferrer's Tigers.[1] They were a death squad that tortured and killed people they captured. There was one Masferrerista in Yara, named Juventino Sutil, who would tie victims up and put them in a sack. Then he'd pour gasoline on them and set them on fire. He killed a number of people this way.

I'll never forget how two compañeras in Yara were raped by the dictatorship's forces: Amelia Puebla, a relative of mine, and Georgina Barbán. They were raped by all the soldiers from the Manzanillo barracks. It was said that about fifty soldiers took part. The two of them subsequently dedicated their lives to the revolution.

1. See glossary, Rolando Masferrer.

Things like this made us join the fight. Just about all the young people in town did so.

We joined the revolutionary movement, determined to take a direct part in the struggle. We didn't come from rich families. We were poor working people. What made us join the struggle were all the abuses, the outrages, the torture, the murders committed by the Batista dictatorship and its henchmen.

WATERS: Yara is famous for the number of combatants it produced. Who were some of the other young people who joined the struggle during those same years?

PUEBLA: They included a number who later became generals in the Revolutionary Armed Forces. There was Harry Villegas, who later fought alongside Che [Guevara] in the Congo and Bolivia. There's General Manuel Lastre, who I went to church and school with. Army Corps General Leopoldo Cintra Frías, an internationalist who's now head of the Western Army. Brigadier General Miguel Lorente, tank commander and internationalist in Ethiopia and Angola. Then there was Flor Pérez Chávez, who was wounded in the battle of Maffo, and Norma Ferrer. And Brig. Gen. Orestes Guerra.

I came to love some of these combatants like brothers. Compañeros like Juan Ramón "Turtó" Figueroa, who was killed in the war, fighting in the Second Front under Commander Raúl Castro. Sometimes I'm asked why I've always maintained close ties to my hometown. It's true that my family still lives there: my mother, my brothers and sisters.

But the truth is, when we left Yara for the Sierra we agreed that if one of us was left alive, that one would continue going home for all of us. That's why I've kept my ties to that town. Not just because I'm from there, but for the memory of those who died in the struggle. It's something I've always felt deeply. We aren't believers in all this stuff about death, but we were compañeros. We go back to the beginning of the war together.

MADRID: What kind of revolutionary work were you involved in when you joined?

PUEBLA: Different activities. Selling bonds to raise money, transporting weapons, helping compañeros get to the Sierra. A host of actions related to the revolutionary war.

Once, on St. Joseph's Day, which is our town's saint's day—March 19, 1957—we went into town and laid down tacks on all the streets. As a result, we flattened the tires of all the cars entering town, carrying out the task of paralyzing the city. On another occasion our objective was to cut the town's power lines.

There was a guard unit consisting of four soldiers in a jeep. They kept crisscrossing the town, which is not very big, so we had to create a diversion. Some of the compañeras said to the soldiers, "Let's go over there and have a soft drink"—far away from the objective.

This enabled the male compañeros to cut the electrical wires.

We sometimes would dress up and use other ruses to carry out our work.

During the 1950s women used to wear a very wide skirt held out with crinolines. It was called "The Deceiver." Under it we'd wear a kind of girdle, into which we'd put the items that needed to be transported. Under that skirt we'd carry bullets, dynamite, or whatever else we were going to transport.

Sometimes too we'd pretend to be pregnant. Nobody would touch the belly of a pregnant woman. But what we were carrying were bullets, messages, dynamite, medicine, and money.

The rich people in town talked about us, of course: "I saw Teté over there, and she was pregnant." They'd see me in another town with a big belly and then suddenly I didn't have a belly anymore. You can imagine what they'd say about us! Or they'd see whites and blacks hanging out together. A white woman with a black man was a problem for them. It became the subject of gossip in a small town like ours.

More important, there was a lot of racial discrimination. Whites lived over here, and the blacks over there. If we went to the park in Manzanillo, for example, blacks used to walk on the inside of the park, and whites on the outside. This was the case wherever you went.

MADRID: What other activities were you involved in?

PUEBLA: I remember one time when Santiago Terry from Havana arrived, trying to get to the mountains. He had been sent to Santiago, and from there to Yara. I calmly got him out of Yara on the back of my bicycle, even though we were surrounded by the town's soldiers. He was able to reach the mountains, where he joined the Rebel Army. At the time of his death in 1986, Terry was a colonel in the Revolutionary Armed Forces.

WATERS: Were there protests or demonstrations by the young people?

PUEBLA: In the bigger cities, yes. But in our small town of Yara, after the war started the army had one of its largest garrisons. An army colonel lived across from my house. So it made the situation in town difficult.

Sometimes we had to transport weapons or other matériel from Yara to another spot. As cover, we used Sergeant del Pino's sons, inviting them to accompany us, to distract attention. Del Pino was one of Batista's henchmen who was later sentenced to thirty years in prison. I used to spend a lot of time with the sergeant's two sons. He didn't know we were in the movement or that his sons were running around with us. And of course they didn't know we were using them.

How did we use them? Each had a girlfriend who was sympathetic to the movement. They weren't members but simply young women who felt they had to do something. Following the *Granma* landing, the army established a garrison in Yara, and closed off the streets. So we used this connection to transport things in and around town. We would have the two women tell del Pino's sons, "Why don't we go to a club somewhere and have a beer? Why don't we go to such-and-such neighborhood in Yara?" So together with the girlfriends and the sergeant's sons, we would all get into their father's jeep—with us carrying the items that needed to be transported. Of course, it wouldn't occur to the soldiers at the checkpoints to stop and search the army's own jeep.

Other times, we would organize a party and invite del Pino's sons over as cover. The party would be going on in one room . . . and we would be making tacks or doing something else in the next room.

We finally reached a point when it was no longer safe to go into town anymore because of the repression. We had to go up to the Sierra.

So with the army on my trail, in July 1957, at the age of sixteen, I went up to the mountains to join the Rebel Army. This in fact had long been my desire, as it was for all revolutionaries at that time, although we couldn't do so as long as we were carrying out useful work in the cities and our identities weren't blown. When I arrived in the Sierra, it was already eight months after the landing of the *Granma* and the uprising in Santiago de Cuba.[2]

2. In November 1956, eighty-two revolutionary combatants—including Fidel Castro, Raúl Castro, Che Guevara, Camilo Cienfuegos, and Juan Almeida—set sail for Cuba aboard the yacht *Granma* from Tuxpan, Mexico. The expeditionaries landed in southeast Cuba on December 2, 1956, marking the beginning of the Cuban

MADRID: Did you go by yourself, or with others? What happened that you had to get out of town?

PUEBLA: A group of compañeros went together. We couldn't remain in the town because a compañero from the July 26 Movement, under torture, had given information, betraying us to the dictatorship. He revealed that we had helped transport weapons from Santiago de Cuba to Manzanillo. So we had no choice but to go up to the mountains.

One of the compañeros who went with me was Rolando Kindelán, who later helped lead the first internationalists in Congo-Brazzaville. There was Ángel Frías, who became a commander in the Rebel Army at the end of the war, and has since passed away. There was also Leonardo and Tony Arias, who were brothers, and were both later killed by Batista's forces.

WATERS: Were there other women who went with you?

PUEBLA: Yes, there were two others: Eugenia Verdecia and Ileana Rodés.

When we reached the rebel camp, the commander in chief greeted us by announcing, "The women have arrived. Now the guerrilla forces are really growing!"

In the Rebel Army

WATERS: Tell us a little about the Rebel Army forces you joined in July 1957, and what you did.

PUEBLA: The Rebel Army wasn't very large in those days. It

---

revolutionary war based in the Sierra Maestra mountains.

Timed originally to coincide with the *Granma* landing, on November 30, 1956, the July 26 Movement in Santiago de Cuba, led by Frank País, staged coordinated attacks on army and police installations, to confront the Batista dictatorship with a general uprising by the population of Santiago. Most of the November 30 combatants joined the Rebel Army in the Sierra Maestra in early 1957.

was a guerrilla unit that moved through the mountains. We were nomads, marching back and forth day and night.

At the beginning, the women were not organized as combatants. We helped with cooking, sewing, and tending for the wounded. We also helped teach the compañeros to read and write. Our guerrilla force during that stage was composed largely of peasants from the Sierra Maestra. The first big group of combatants was mainly townspeople, but peasants from the region had started to join, among them some who had supported the rebels from the beginning. So the Rebel Army began teaching them how to read and write. The first Rebel Army literacy teacher was Che, who taught Joel Iglesias and Alejandro Oñate, who was nicknamed "Cantinflas."

I remember that whenever a letter arrived for a compañero who couldn't read, we'd read it to him. We'd also write letters for these compañeros, based on what they'd dictate to us. Afterwards we began teaching them to read and write, using a little notebook.

Various compañeras gave classes to the rebel combatants. We also established little schools for the peasants' children. Women teachers who had belonged to the July 26 Movement in the cities came and worked in these schools. They would join the Rebel Army and start teaching classes.

In the latter stages of the war, we set up schools in the Sierra. And we'd teach reading and writing to the rebels, the peasants, and the peasants' children. Garment and weapons fabrication workshops were organized, and there was the school for recruits at Minas del Frío. There people were taught equally how to handle weapons and how to read and write.[3]

3. In April 1958 the Rebel Army set up a school for recruits in Minas del Frío in the Sierra Maestra. Its first head was Ernesto Che Guevara.

Women also worked in the hospitals. We helped the doctors treat the wounded. We went on missions to get medicines. We were couriers. In other words, women did just about everything. But what each of us really wanted was to obtain a rifle. And when we were finally given rifles, we demonstrated we could fight.

Celia Sánchez

WATERS: Celia Sánchez was one of the leaders of the July 26 Movement in Oriente who had to go up to the Sierra early on in the revolutionary war. Did you get to know and work with her?

PUEBLA: When I got to the Sierra, Celia Sánchez was there. She was the connection with the urban underground. I arrived while she was away. She'd gone off on a mission.

Celia organized everything. She was the one who would decide where to put the hospital or how to improve it, which small school we would open.

When you speak of Celia, you've got to speak of Fidel, and vice versa. Celia's ideas touched almost everything in the Sierra. She was the soul of the Sierra Maestra, very capable, yet very sensitive to the needs of others. She never had a harsh word for even the worst enemy of the revolution. She was loved by all. Those of us who were guerrilla fighters consider her the mother of the Rebel Army, because of her firmness and loyalty, because of the way she conducted herself during the war.

In the Sierra Celia was in charge of just about everything, not only the hospitals and schools, but the general command post, which was established in 1958. She was also in charge of the sewing shops, the armory, the transport of goods, messengers. If a woman was giving birth in the mountains, or if a peasant was ill and it was necessary to take medicine to them,

Celia was in charge of it. After the revolution's triumph she maintained these concerns. I was always near Celia, until the end of her life. She was the most humane, unassuming person there was.

Celia truly influenced our entire people. Peasants from the Sierra Maestra talk about her as someone who's very dear to them, someone who they consider to be their own, like a beloved member of their own family whose memory is still alive.

MADRID: You mentioned the sewing shop and armory that Celia helped establish. What were they?

PUEBLA: The garment shop in the Sierra made the rebels' uniforms. They were of very poor quality, but the most important thing was we were able to make uniforms. The armory was set up because we didn't have enough weapons and had to reuse the same bombs that were dropped on us; all unexploded bombs were taken to the bomb workshop. There they made the M-26s, which we also called "Sputniks." The M-26 was an explosive fired from a type of catapult, made from a rifle. The charge came from bombs dropped by the dictatorship that didn't go off. Batista's soldiers were terrified of it.

This same armory also made mines, which we laid for the tanks whenever they came up into the mountains, or elsewhere. If one of those mines exploded under a tank, that was it for the tank. We didn't have any other weapons to use against tanks.

Che Guevara

MARTÍN KOPPEL: You became a member of Che Guevara's column for a while. How did that come about?

PUEBLA: In November 1957 I got sick, with a very high fever, and Dr. Martínez Páez decided I should stay back and recuperate in Che's camp at El Hombrito.[4] When Che saw me, he was very concerned. He asked how I felt, whether I was getting better, what treatment I was getting. Right away I could see how humane he was. He treated everyone that way.

In addition to being a combatant and commander, Che carried out his duties as doctor. Whenever a compañero was wounded, he personally took responsibility for treating them. If someone had a headache, he would try to find out what was wrong with that compañero, looking for the root of the problem and its solution. One thing he enjoyed was pulling teeth whenever someone had a toothache. The peasants would look for him day and night. He even delivered babies in the Sierra Maestra.

He was also a teacher; he himself taught a number of compañeros and he was concerned that everyone who didn't know how to read and write should learn to do so. And not just the Rebel Army combatants, but the peasants as well.

Che was attentive to everyone's personal problems. If someone had a family situation, he would try to help resolve it. He couldn't stand to see anyone sad. He would immediately try to find the causes, and resolve them, if that were possible. There was something in his personality that made him stand out among his compañeros.

To the troops he was like a father or an older brother. He established relations of respect and discipline, combined with very fraternal affection. This explains why his men admired and loved him very much and why they were ready to fulfill any mission he gave them.

4. In July 1957 the Rebel Army set up a second column in the eastern part of the Sierra Maestra, commanded by Che Guevara. Its base was El Hombrito, where it established workshops, a hospital, and a school.

While I was at El Hombrito, the battle of Mar Verde was fought, in which Ciro Redondo was killed. When Che returned he met with us to inform us of the results of that action. When he referred to those killed, his eyes filled with tears. This made a very big impression on me, seeing a great warrior who was capable of tears in face of the loss of a good fighter and friend.

I remember also that he was a man who loved poetry. On cold, rainy days when we couldn't march, he would read poems. I don't know if they were his or others, but I do know he loved poetry.

In December 1957 I returned to Fidel's column, and I didn't see Che again until the dictatorship's offensive in mid-1958.

A dangerous mission

MADRID: What happened during this offensive?

PUEBLA: In May 1958 Batista's army launched an offensive by 10,000 soldiers against our 300 rebels in the Sierra. And we had even fewer weapons, not more than 200, and some of these were not regular weapons but arms like the M-26 that I described earlier, which we made in the Sierra. But we defeated them, inflicting many casualties, taking many prisoners—some soldiers let themselves be captured several times—and in July they finally had to withdraw.[5]

As the offensive was ending, I participated in handing over

5. In late May 1958 the Batista army launched an "encircle and annihilate" offensive. The Rebel Army concentrated some of its forces to confront the troops of the dictatorship. By the time the army's offensive had been beaten in July 1958, the Rebel Army had inflicted over 1,000 casualties on Batista's forces, had grown to 800 combatants and had captured 600 weapons. Building on the momentum of this victory, the Rebel Army went on the offensive, which culminated with the revolution's victory on January 1, 1959.

captured Batista soldiers to the International Red Cross.

WATERS: What was your mission?

PUEBLA: We had taken several hundred prisoners, and there were too few of us to care for that many people. So Fidel wrote a letter to the International Red Cross proposing that these prisoners be handed over to them. He addressed the letter to the Red Cross here in Cuba and not the Batista government. To accomplish the handover, a truce with Batista's army was needed. The dictatorship didn't want to accept a truce, because by doing so they'd be acknowledging having been defeated. But the International Red Cross agreed.

It was decided that I would be the messenger to establish the truce. I was seventeen years old at the time. I was chosen because if a man were sent, he would have been killed. If a woman went, they might not shoot her.

Our estimation was that because of my age, and the fact that I was not an ugly young woman at the time, the army would agree to the truce and not shoot the rebel messenger.

Che spoke to me about this.

"All right Teté," he said, "three things can happen. They can accept the truce and everything's fine. Or they can kill you." That is, they could shoot me before I reached them. "Or they can take you prisoner and bring you to Bayamo."

"Well, the truce has to be arranged in any event," I told Che, "and I'm willing to do it."

So we washed and ironed my one olive green uniform, and at 5:30 or 6:00 a.m., I left from Altos de Mompié.

I went on a mule, carrying a white flag, unarmed and accompanied by a peasant from the area. I let down my long hair, and was wearing a July 26 Movement armband. I was going down from the heights of the Sierra Maestra, toward an area dominated by Batista's soldiers. We were located along the upper ridge of the Sierra Maestra, and Batista's army controlled the lower portions.

We calculated that it would take about two and a half hours, that I'd get there around 8:30 and be back around noon. But on the way down their aircraft started bombing, and I had to try and protect myself from the shrapnel. In the process the mule got away, and I had to continue on foot. So I didn't get there until noon. As I approached, I waved a white handkerchief, so the troops wouldn't shoot.

At the first army post, they told me to halt and asked me what I wanted. I told them I was bringing a message from our general command post for their commanding officer. With threatening looks on their faces, they told me to give it to them. I said no. They took me to their commanding officer, Captain Durán Batista.

I then had to wait for Major Merob Sosa, who was in Bayamo, to return to Las Vegas de Jibacoa. Merob Sosa was one of the bloodiest officers the dictatorship had. He was the one I had to give Che's message to.

In that letter, Che asked them for a truce to allow the prisoners to be handed over. I still have that letter.

After reading the letter, Durán Batista said to me: "You have to take that armband off." Moreover, he added, "We've told the troops that the ones being handed over are rebels."

I responded: "The soldiers have to know that it's not rebels who are being handed over. Every last one of us will die fighting in the Sierra rather than surrender. And I can't take this armband off. You couldn't understand its meaning—it's the symbol of our struggle."

He talked about taking me to Bayamo. He was insulting and asked me how a pretty girl like me could be with that bedraggled and filthy bunch. He told me that the war was just about over and that they were winning it. I answered that this wasn't true, and I reminded him that the ones we were handing over were government troops, not rebels.

They agreed to the truce!

It was around 6:00 p.m. when I got back. Our people thought the worst had happened, because I was supposed to be back at noon. They were very worried. Seeing me made a big impression on our forces. When I got back to the command post, I noticed that Fidel, Che, and Camilo, along with all our people, were there waiting for me. They tossed me on their shoulders joyfully from one person to the next. They were so happy to see me back and unharmed. And they were happy with the positive response from Batista's officers.

That same night they told me I had to go back.

I took the response drafted by Che to Captain Durán Batista.

I got to the army's camp at ten o'clock at night. I was told to halt. I explained the same thing as the last time, that I was bearing a message from our general command post for their commanding officer. They let me through and brought me to the hut where Captain Durán Batista was. I gave him the message.

At all costs Durán Batista wanted to prevent me from talking to the soldiers. He gave me his cot, and he laid down in a hammock next to it, so he could keep an eye on me. Being among Batista's soldiers I could not go to sleep. I waited until the captain fell asleep, and then I sneaked away and began talking to the soldiers in the trenches. I told them that the ones to be handed over were captured soldiers. I stated again and again during those hours that all the rebels would fight to the death in the Sierra. They later said that this was the safest night they'd had in the mountains, knowing that the rebels wouldn't attack while I was there.

"How many weapons do you all have, and how many of you are there?" I was asked. Then as a test, they'd show me

SIERRA MAESTRA, JULY 22, 1958

TO THE COMMANDER ASSIGNED
TO THE POST AT LAS VEGAS

Sir:

It is my duty to inform you that, as agreed to by the International Red Cross, we are handing over to you this afternoon the first batch of wounded prisoners. The bearer of this letter, compañera Teté Puebla, a member of our army's health and sanitation service, is assigned to inform you of the final measures we have taken in this regard.

At 2:00 p.m., as long as there are no bombings during the hours that have become customary—if there are, this will delay by several hours the handover of the prisoners—they will be in territory under your military command. I should warn you that the house where we will make the handover belongs to a man whose first name is Bismark (we don't know his last name). This house is situated some 500 meters from your customary positions, and that's where the delegate from the International Red Cross should go, with his corresponding documents. The stretcher-bearers and officers can accompany him if they wish, with or without weapons, but always under that institution's guarantees.

The heights overlooking the house we have chosen will be dominated by our forces. They will not permit the troops under your command to advance toward their positions. Doing so will be considered by us to be a violation of the truce.

The handover of the prisoners will not be made un-

> til we receive an affirmative response to the plan proposed signed by a responsible person, and given to the same messenger. Any outrage committed against our messenger will lead to the breakoff of negotiations, and therefore of the truce imposed on this part of the battle front.
>
> I shall communicate to the delegate of the International Red Cross that you will be ready to receive, probably tomorrow, a new group of wounded. The seriousness of their wounds does not permit their being jostled during transport, since they have undergone emergency surgery. We will soon be able to give you the number of these wounded.
>
> Greetings,
> s/CHE
> Commander of "Ciro Redondo" Column no. 8

weapons and ask me to identify them. Fortunately, I knew how to handle all those weapons, even though I hadn't used them in combat.

Finally, the International Red Cross arrived and I was able to return with their response.

Then Che and Faustino Pérez came down, together with the prisoners—over 200 of them marching in single file, exhausted and demoralized. Many supported themselves with canes made of branches, or on the shoulders of their comrades. We carried those most seriously wounded on hammocks.

From the doors or windows of their huts, peasants watched the strange caravan pass by; it was something they'd never seen before. They watched with a mixture of pity for the prisoners combined with joy, because the prisoners marching

GRANMA

Rebel Army combatants assist members of International Red Cross during handover of wounded Batista army soldiers, July 1958.

SIERRA MAESTRA, JULY 22, 1958

CAPTAIN CARLOS DURÁN BATISTA
LAS VEGAS DE JIBACOA

Dear captain:

With urgency, I am answering your note of earlier today. . . . I will send the most seriously wounded without awaiting the arrival of the International Red Cross.

These wounded are quite a distance from that point, and given the poor condition of the roads in the Sierra, I cannot state ahead of time the exact hour when they will arrive. . . . Be assured, I repeat, that we will strictly observe the truce. We nevertheless want to know exactly when it will go until. . . . We require 48 hours beginning from the arrival of the delegate from the International Red Cross, announced by radio for 2:00 p.m. tomorrow. . . .

On the express order of our commander in chief, Fidel Castro, we will deliver, in addition to the wounded, all the survivors of the 18th Infantry Battalion led by Major Quevedo, who surrendered to our forces. . . .

If possible, we would prefer to leave our messenger at that spot so she can inform us rapidly when the delegate from the International Red Cross arrives. . . .

Wishing to shake your hand in the happiest circumstances for Cuba,

COMMANDER OF "CIRO REDONDO" COLUMN 8

by were symbols of the hated regime, of its outrages and crimes.

When they arrived, we started turning over our prisoners. Even though they belonged to Batista's army, a rapport had developed between our troops and the prisoners, to the point that right then you didn't know who were soldiers and who were rebels.

At that moment we were all Cubans, even though we were fighting for the people and our revolution, while they were defending a dictatorship that was murdering and destroying.

There were even cases where brother met brother and cousin met cousin, each in a different army. That was very moving. This was the first truce that had been arranged with the army of the tyranny. It lasted about 48 hours.

During that time we handed over 253 prisoners, 57 of them wounded.

After my assignment as a messenger to establish the truce, I was sent to Santiago de Cuba three times to open up new lines of communication. We lacked food and medicines, and the broadcasting equipment for Radio Rebelde wasn't working. I made these trips before the creation of the Marianas. But what we wanted more than anything was to earn the right to fight.

The Mariana Grajales Women's Platoon

Waters: The founding of the Mariana Grajales Women's Platoon marked a milestone in the Cuban Revolution. It demonstrated in practice the social course a victorious Rebel Army would fight for. As Karl Marx put it, you can judge any society by the status of women.

What led to the unit's formation?

Puebla: In May 1958, as the dictatorship's military offensive began, the army stepped up its repression against the population of the Sierra Maestra. Wherever the army went, women were raped, children were killed, entire villages were bombed and burned down. Peasants had to leave the Sierra. Sánchez Mosquera was one of the most infamous of Batista's commanders, but there were others.

They would announce they'd killed a lot of Rebel Army soldiers. But that wasn't true; the people killed were peasants. They were dragged out of their huts at gunpoint. They used to tie the men to poles while raping the women. Then they'd kill everyone. Whole families would be wiped out.

They were bombing villages, too. One of these was Cayo Espino, which was of no military value. Our commander has spoken about this, but for those of us who were there these crimes affected us deeply, they outraged everybody. There was a five-year-old boy named Orestes Gutiérrez in Cayo Espino. His legs were blown off by one of the bombs, and other members of his family were wounded. Everyone in the Sierra knew the story of this little boy, who told his grandmother, holding her hand: "Grandmother, I won't be able to love you anymore because I'm going to die." His grandfather died too. His two sisters were wounded, but they are alive today thanks to the Rebel Army doctors who gave them immediate attention. And the bombing was done in an area where there were no rebel troops.

Throughout the region of Oro de Guisa, peasant houses were set afire. The peasants who fled the flames were seized, and then raped or killed. All these crimes filled us with courage and determination. Even though we were doing many essential things, we felt frustrated that we could not fight arms in hand. "They've got to let us fight," we said.

We had already proved that women could do just about everything. We withstood the bombings, delivered weapons, and were in the places where fighting was taking place. But we were still not allowed to fight.

"If women have to take part in all the duties of the revolution," we said, "why can't we fight for the revolution in the same way as our men fight?"

After the army's offensive had been defeated, we asked our commander in chief to allow us to fight arms in hand. He agreed. Fidel said yes, women had won the right to fight with a rifle face to face with the enemy.

On September 4, 1958, a meeting took place, a sort of roundtable. Fidel assembled his general staff at the time, those who were left in the Sierra Maestra. The invasion troops—Columns 2 and 8 under the command of Camilo Cienfuegos and Ernesto Che Guevara—had already left. And a Second and a

> On Thursday, April 10, after the clash at Pozón—in which a detachment of the dictatorship that had left Yara to pursue a rebel patrol that had attacked a convoy on the Manzanillo-Bayamo road was completely wiped out—three B-26s, a jet, and two light planes ruthlessly attacked the rural village of Cayo Espino, where there are no military objectives, for two hours. Every home in the town was hit by the planes' fire. A field hospital was improvised in the rear with three doctors from the July 26 Movement to care for the wounded, who had to wait for nightfall before they could be moved. A five-year-old child lost a lot of blood on the way and died on an improvised operating table, his legs torn off by a .50-caliber bullet fired from a plane that also wounded his two little sisters.
>
> FIDEL CASTRO, APRIL 15, 1958

Third Front had already been established in Oriente.[1]

There was a discussion at this roundtable meeting that lasted more than seven hours. Fidel had a very big argument there. There were still not enough weapons for everyone, and the men were saying, "How can we give rifles to women when there are so many men who are unarmed?"

Fidel answered: "Because they're better soldiers than you are. They're more disciplined."

1. In March 1958 the Rebel Army founded a Second and Third Front, led by Raúl Castro and Juan Almeida respectively, to extend the war from the Sierra Maestra to the rest of Oriente province (see map on page 23). In the following months two new columns were formed to undertake a westward "invasion" of Cuba's central and eastern provinces. These were Column 8 led by Ernesto Che Guevara and Column 2 commanded by Camilo Cienfuegos.

"In any event," he said, "I'm going to put together the squad, and I'm going to teach them how to shoot."

So on September 4, the Mariana Grajales Women's Platoon was formed. As I explained, Isabel Rielo became the commanding officer. I was named second in command. The squad came to have thirteen combatants in it. The commander in chief chose the name as a tribute to Mariana Grajales, a heroine of our war of independence and the mother of Antonio Maceo, the legendary general who fought heroically in Cuba's wars of independence for over thirty years.

Fidel was the one who taught us to shoot. We had to hit a quarter—or a 20-centavo coin—20 to 30 meters away, depending on how he wanted to test our aim. And he drilled us. We had to split that coin.

In fact, Isabel Rielo was named the commanding officer as a result of target practice. Because she was a better shot than I was. Fidel had said that whoever was the best shot would be named head of the platoon.

It was decided that the M-1 was to be our weapon, because it was lighter. Fidel ordered that everyone in our squad be supplied with that rifle. Nevertheless he didn't drill us with the M-1; he made us practice with the Garand and other, heavier guns. He'd say that the M-1 was easier to use, but that we needed to be able to fire any kind of rifle. Once we had learned to shoot, the last thing we practiced with was the M-1.

Then Fidel informed us: "You're now going to be my personal security detail."

From that day on, when people saw us, they would comment: "The Marianas are here. Our commander in chief must be arriving." We were his advance detachment. He did this to demonstrate his confidence in women, in women's equality.

Some of the other men would say things like, "If the enemy

> The Mariana Grajales Squad of rebel women went into action for the first time in this battle and firmly held its ground under shelling from the Sherman tanks.
>
> FIDEL CASTRO, OCTOBER 1958

soldiers toss a lizard at them, the women are going to dump their rifles and run." But they were jealous, because Fidel used to say, "They're better soldiers than you are."

MADRID: Did the platoon include all the women in the mountains?

PUEBLA: No, there were other compañeras serving as nurses in the hospitals, as teachers, in the garment shops. The Mariana Grajales Platoon was made up of women in the Sierra who wanted to join a combat unit.

The first combat we saw was the battle of Cerro Pelado on September 27, 1958. This was the Marianas' baptism by fire. The entire squad participated.

This was a tough battle. Remember that the enemy had artillery. The area had become the last redoubt of the dictatorship's troops who had fled the territory after our counteroffensive had begun. We had to fight to get them out of the Sierra Maestra. Five compañeros were killed in the fighting; there were no casualties among the Marianas. Fidel has talked about this battle.

Afterward, Fidel went up to Eddy Suñol, one of the officers who was most opposed to having us as combatants, and he said: "I have a mission for you. We want to send you down to the plains, but you're going to take the girls with you."

Right then and there Commander Suñol said no. "I'm not going to the cities with them."

Frankly, he was forced to take us. Fidel told him: "Either

FUERZAS ARMADAS REVOLUCIONARIAS

Fidel Castro with members of the Mariana Grajales Platoon, 1958. Left to right: Lola Feria, Edemis Tamayo, Teté Puebla, Fidel Castro, Isabel Rielo, Celia Sánchez, Lilia Rielo, Eddy Suñol.

> I have to tell you that after having been one of the main opponents of women's integration, I'm now completely satisfied. I congratulate you once again because you are never wrong. Beforehand I believed that this time you were mistaken. I wish you could see—even if it were a movie, so you could smile with joy—the actions of Teté in particular, as well as the other compañeras. When the order was given to advance, some of the men stayed behind, but the women went ahead in the vanguard. Their courage and calmness merits the respect and admiration of all the rebels and everyone else.
>
> EDDY SUÑOL
>
> Letter to Fidel Castro, October 1958

you take the women or you're not going." Suñol took us, although he did so gritting his teeth.

We arrived in Holguín on the night of October 20. The first battle began at dawn on the 21st, near the Holguín reservoir, where we were surprised by two trucks and a jeep full of the dictatorship's soldiers.

We were surrounded with no way out, because the soldiers were less than ten minutes away from us. We agreed among ourselves that we would never surrender. We'd die fighting.

WATERS: The army troops must have been surprised to see you.

PUEBLA: Yes, because they had never before seen women in combat.

Back at the command post, when the report on the battle was made, the question was asked: "How did the women conduct themselves? What was their stance?" After that battle, the issue was settled. Women could fight alongside the men.

Radio Rebelde was reporting it. We suffered two wounded and captured eleven rifles.

MADRID: What about Eddy Suñol?

PUEBLA: Suñol sent a message to Fidel apologizing for having opposed him on this question and acknowledging that Fidel was right. Because that battle had demonstrated that what Fidel had been saying about women was correct. They are as good soldiers as the men.

MADRID: Did all thirteen of you participate in the fighting in Holguín?

PUEBLA: No, only four of us left with Commander Eddy Suñol because the squad was divided up. The other group remained at the command post and later participated in the battles of Guisa and Maffo, both of which were led by Fidel.

Fidel's idea was to create two women's units, but the war ended before that could happen.

A few days later, the Marianas saw combat again, this time at the head of the troops.

This was the battle of Los Güiros, on November 2. It took place along the highway on the day of the elections, to obstruct the elections and the movement of troops.[2]

That too was a very intense battle. Suñol, our commander, was wounded and the other officers who were there had to get him out. The road was very narrow. Compañera Isabel, who was a medic, went to rescue him, together with compañero Omar Iser Mojena and compañero Flavio Quesada. So we were left alone to lead the battle. I ended up in charge of

2. The Batista regime had organized general elections for November 3, 1958, in an attempt to provide a legal cover to the dictatorship. The July 26 Movement called for a boycott and organized actions to obstruct the elections. Amid massive voter abstention, Batista's candidate for president, Andrés Rivero Agüero, was declared elected.

> Near Holguín, a woman's platoon engaged in a fierce battle with the army and the platoon leader was wounded. As a general rule, when a platoon leader was wounded the men had the habit of retreating—which is not correct but it had become practically a habit. The women's platoon had attacked a truck loaded with soldiers. When the platoon leader was wounded, they weren't discouraged. They went on fighting, wiped out the truckload, and captured all the weapons. Their behavior was truly exceptional.
>
> FIDEL CASTRO, JANUARY 20, 1981

the troops since I was the ranking combatant.

WATERS: Rescuing wounded fighters was always a principle of the Rebel Army, wasn't it?

PUEBLA: Yes. If a rebel was captured, the dictatorship's army would do terrible things to him. They would gouge out his eyes and cut off his private parts. So we never left any rebel behind who might be taken prisoner. Speaking for myself, I kept a bullet for this purpose—I still hold onto it. Lilia Rielo and I made a blood pact that if either of us were wounded, without possibilities of getting out alive or in danger of falling prisoner, the other one would prevent these tortures by using the bullet.

Because if the dictatorship's army had taken any of us prisoner, they'd have raped and tortured us for sure. I said to myself: No way!

Not only did we not leave our wounded behind; to the extent possible we always took our dead.

MADRID: What impact did the wounding of Suñol have on the rebel forces?

PUEBLA: It was a blow, but in spite of that the platoon didn't fall apart. As the commander in chief later said, "When their commanding officer was wounded, the women stayed at the front."

KOPPEL: How many Marianas participated?

PUEBLA: There were four of us, and nearly all of the enemy soldiers were taken prisoner. We grabbed up all their weapons.

It was quite a surprise for them that we were the ones who took them prisoner.

In 1998, after the fortieth anniversary ceremony in Holguín marking the founding of the Fourth Front, led by Delio Gómez Ochoa, we met one of the soldiers we took prisoner there. At this activity I spoke on behalf of our front. When I'd finished, there was a compañero waiting for me. He asked, "Don't you know me, Teté?" I said no, and he replied, "I'm the kepi." Compañera Lilia Rielo was also there, and we both burst out laughing. A journalist came over and asked, "Why are you laughing so hard?"

The story is that during the battle at Los Güiros we had taken a soldier prisoner. At the point we were trying to withdraw, planes began strafing us and we all took cover under some bushes. But this soldier refused to hide.

So we yelled at him, "Casquito, casquito, come here." *Casquito* [little helmet] was the derogatory term we used for Batista's soldiers, because of the headgear they wore. And he answered, "No, no, I'm not coming." We cursed at him. I won't repeat the curseword we used. Then he said, "And besides, I'm not a casquito. I'm a kepi." A kepi was the military cap worn by noncommissioned officers instead of helmets. Corporals and sergeants, who got higher pay in Batista's army, never wanted to be confused with privates. This was why he took so long obeying our command to protect himself from

> It has been proven that not only men can fight, but in Cuba women also fight. The best evidence of this is the Mariana Grajales Platoon, which so distinguished itself in numerous battles. Women make excellent soldiers, as good as our best male soldiers, and I wanted to demonstrate that.
>
> At the beginning, the idea involved a lot of effort for me because there was a lot of prejudice. There were men who asked how could we give a rifle to a woman when there was still a man available. Within our ranks, women remain a layer that needs to be freed, because they are still victims of discrimination on the job and in other aspects of life.
>
> So we organized the women's unit. They demonstrated that women can fight. A people whose women fight alongside men—that people is invincible. . . .
>
> We will organize female combatants or militias, we will keep them trained—all of them on a voluntary basis. And to all the young women I see here with their dresses draped in the red and black colors of the July 26 Movement, I ask you to learn how to handle weapons.
>
> FIDEL CASTRO, SANTIAGO DE CUBA, JANUARY 2, 1959

the plane's bullets. Finally he did so.

We all laughed as we remembered this, and we had to explain it to everyone else around. This casquito, by the way, is now a member of the Communist Party of Cuba, a builder of socialism.

WATERS: How did the attitude toward you of the men who were combatants change?

PUEBLA: As these battles took place, the men were able to see how we fought alongside them. We never fell behind. We were always beside or ahead of them. There was no difference. And this was difficult combat, because none of our weapons had much ammunition.

So Cuban women earned our renown as combatants. Fidel likes to say that the Mariana Grajales Platoon was the forerunner, setting the example of women defending our homeland.

WATERS: Where were you when the revolution triumphed on January 1, 1959?

PUEBLA: We were in Bayamo at the time, where I participated in a number of actions right up to the triumph. Then Fidel sent for us to join the Liberty Caravan.[3]

Isabel Rielo and I both finished the war with the rank of first lieutenant, and there were also five lieutenants. I was promoted to captain May 24, 1959.

When the war was over, in his speech of January 2, 1959, Fidel said, "A country where men and women can both fight—that's an invincible people."

After 43 years of revolution Fidel is still saying the same thing. He has always been the strongest supporter and defender of women.

3. In face of the Rebel Army's military victories and a growing popular uprising, Fulgencio Batista fled Cuba on January 1, 1959. A U.S.-sponsored attempt to replace Batista with another military officer and forestall the victory of the Rebel Army was defeated through a nationwide general strike called by Fidel Castro on behalf of the Rebel Army and July 26 Movement and through the swift advance on Havana by the columns led by Che Guevara and Camilo Cienfuegos. The main columns of the Rebel Army then traveled from Santiago de Cuba to Havana January 2–8 in a Liberty Caravan, organizing mass mobilizations in Cuba's main cities as they went. The caravan entered Havana on January 8, receiving a tumultuous welcome by the city's population.

COURTESY TETÉ PUEBLA

Members of the Mariana Grajales Platoon outside Havana, January 1959. Left to right: Olga Guevara, Ada Bella Acosta, Isabel Rielo, Teté Puebla, Lilia Rielo.

Social solidarity: the moral foundation of the revolution

Waters: Fidel has often said that as difficult as it was to overthrow the Batista regime, the much bigger challenges began after January 1, 1959. The Rebel Army and July 26 Movement had to lead working people to take the political power they had won, to transform social relations from top to bottom, and to defend the revolution from attack by the U.S. ruling class and its government.

What new tasks did you find yourself responsible for after the revolution's triumph?

Puebla: On January 8, 1959, as we were heading to our homes, thinking of catching a few days' rest, the commander said to me: "You're going to tend to Oriente province," to head up the Department of Assistance to War Victims and Their Families, which was led by the Rebel Army in the area. We had to deal with all those affected by all the dictatorship's crimes, the burned-down houses, the destruction from the offensives waged in the eastern region. The new department's slogan was, "In the face of pain, the homeland makes no distinction. To save a child is to build the homeland."

So in early 1959 I went to Oriente province, to see to the victims of the war and their families. We worked very closely with Celia and Fidel on this. The work began on February 4 that year.

This was very satisfying work. Of all the things I've done in my life, this is one I'm proudest of: helping all these people.

Taking care of the victims of war was a tradition of ours going back to the days of the Sierra Maestra.

An example is the case of Eutimio Guerra, a peasant who joined the struggle and helped in the early days. But he turned traitor and sold out to the dictatorship's army for money. His assignment was to kill Fidel, but he was discovered and executed. Afterward we took care of his family. They were given 50 pesos a month, even though our guerrilla column had no money. And we gave them a cow, so his children would be fed. His widow and four children became fully incorporated into the revolutionary process.

So in Oriente our starting point was to take care of all the victims of the war. We addressed everything the Batista government had destroyed.

Sometimes you'd care for a peasant child whose mother and father had been murdered, whose house had been burned down. And since our army is an army of the people, we rebuilt all those houses that Batista's army had burned down. We took in all these families because they'd had their land taken away, they'd lost their jobs, they'd suffered every kind of abuse.

The Masferreristas—the ones I referred to earlier who would put people in a sack, pour gasoline on them, and burn them alive—those perverted assassins were in all the eastern zones, and they devastated towns.

But the families of these murderers were provided for. Their children were provided for the same as the children of the rebels. That's why with all truthfulness we can say our revolution is so great and humane. Although we had no money, we provided their children with the same care and the same schools that we provided to the rebels' children. The children, the mothers, the widows weren't to blame for the murders the army of the dictatorship committed. So we looked after them in the same way. Batista soldiers' widows along with rebel fighters' widows attended schools for adults.

MADRID: Were there some who didn't want to do this?

PUEBLA: We all accepted these instructions. We said: "If the commander says this is how a real revolution acts, that's how it must be."

One of the things we did in Oriente was build schools for the orphans, as well as foster homes. We named these after martyrs of our revolution, those who had fallen in battle. This was a tradition of ours going back to the Sierra Maestra. In the village of Santo Domingo where I was during the war, for example, we named our little school after Pastor Palomares, a compañero who had been killed in combat.

Among the people there was a great deal of hatred for the murderers of Batista's army, and everyone knew who the killers were. So whenever we set up a school with a group of children, we didn't say who their parents were. Only those of us in charge of them knew. We protected these children in this way. At present those boys and girls are doctors, engineers, university graduates. They're part of the revolution. There are eighteen war orphans that are like my own children to me, and their children are like my grandchildren.

The widows and mothers of members of the Batista army collect a pension, and that's been true throughout the 43 years of our revolutionary process.

This is a characteristic of the revolution. It's called humanity. Love for one's fellow human being. Love for the family, for the people, for countries that suffer injustice. We identify with all peoples of the world who fight against misery and hunger. We feel the same way for the hundreds of millions of abandoned children in the world who live in the streets

COURTESY TETÉ PUEBLA

Celia Sánchez (left) and Teté Puebla in 1979, shortly before Sánchez's death, at a reception for peasant collaborators of the Rebel Army.

looking for the means to subsist on. There are no such children here in Cuba. Because even back then in those penniless times, this revolution was capable of sheltering everyone, of taking these children off the streets. If the revolution didn't have these qualities, it would no longer exist. This began with Fidel. These principles of the revolution are the moral foundation of our struggle.

WATERS: After the initial years, how did this work continue?

PUEBLA: First we saw to all the consequences of the war. Then came the Escambray and Girón.[1] And we saw to all the families of those murdered in the Escambray during the struggle against the bandits. But we also helped the families of the assassins themselves. We placed their children in schools. Their wives and mothers were helped in every way. They didn't end up in the street.

In August 1964 I was transferred to Havana and put in charge of the Children's Farms for war orphans, and for Social Security within the Western Army. I had this assignment until 1966.

MADRID: What were the Children's Farms?

PUEBLA: These were actually schools for war orphans that we called farms. The children who went to those schools were the children of rebels as well as the children of Batista's

1. The Escambray mountains of south-central Cuba was the main scene of operations of a battle the Cuban Revolution waged between 1959 and 1965 against CIA-armed and -financed counterrevolutionary bands.

Playa Girón on the Bay of Pigs, just west of the Escambray, was the site of an invasion by some 1,500 U.S.-organized and -supplied mercenary troops in April 1961. The invasion was defeated within 72 hours.

See glossary, Playa Girón; Struggle against bandits.

troops. Remember that the department's motto was: "In the face of suffering, the homeland helps all."

Schools were built in all the provinces. Here in Havana schools were named after Ciro Frías, Ramón Paz, Osvaldo Herrera, and other compañeros killed in the war. In Holguín I couldn't decide what to call it—all of the compañeros were dear to me—so I named it Martyrs of the Revolution. The idea was to honor not just one single compañero, but many.

In April 1966 I was transferred to the general staff and served in a special unit led by Sergio del Valle to attend to the needs of the families of those who had left to fulfill internationalist missions.

So I've been doing this since the first Cuban volunteers left for Algeria, for the Congo, Vietnam, Angola, Ethiopia, everywhere.[2] I've been helping all their families, so they wouldn't

2. In 1963 Cuban troops went to Algeria, at the request of the revolutionary government of Ahmed Ben Bella, to combat an imperialist-inspired invasion of that country by Morocco.

In 1965 Cuban volunteers led by Che Guevara fought alongside national liberation forces in the Congo against U.S.-backed Belgian and South African mercenaries. (See Víctor Dreke, *From the Escambray to the Congo: In the Whirlwind of the Cuban Revolution* [Pathfinder, 2002], for a first-hand account by the second in command of the operation, working under Che Guevara.)

During Vietnam's war of national liberation against U.S. aggression during the 1960s and 1970s, Cuban internationalist volunteers extended their cooperation. Among these volunteers was a Cuban military construction unit that helped the Vietnamese build the so-called Ho Chi Minh Trail that helped supply liberation fighters in South Vietnam.

Between 1975 and 1989, more than 300,000 Cuban internationalist combatants served in Angola, helping to defend that country against a South African invasion and an imperialist-backed insurgency supported by Washington, among others.

In 1977 Cuba responded to a request by the government of Ethiopia to help defeat a U.S.-backed invasion by the regime in neigh-

have to worry about any situation that might arise. Later on, I also oversaw the care of all the physically disabled who served on internationalist missions.

When we go to these countries, we don't take their wealth or resources home with us. The only material thing we bring back to Cuba is our dead. The compañeros who fell fulfilling internationalist missions didn't die in vain. They died for the revolution, to defend the principles of our revolution, aiding movements that had requested our help in different parts of the world.

boring Somalia aimed at seizing the Ogaden region. Washington planned to use a Somali victory as a springboard to help turn back land redistribution and other measures that had been taken in Ethiopia following the overthrow of the landlord-based monarchy of Emperor Haile Selassie in 1974.

Opening the doors to women's social equality

WATERS: Around the world, many are interested in your story because it helps capture what the Cuban Revolution has meant for women. What have been some of the biggest changes?

PUEBLA: The first great effort was the literacy drive, which had its roots in the Rebel Army. There was a department for this in the armed forces.

In 1958 I helped Celia organize elementary schools in the Sierra Maestra, since there were none there, and of course many children were illiterate. The big majority of peasant women were illiterate, and many rebel fighters too.

Cuba was the first in the world to eradicate illiteracy.[1] Women were part of that struggle, young women especially. There was a massive incorporation of youth and children

1. From late 1960 through 1961, the revolutionary government undertook a drive to wipe out illiteracy. Central to this effort to teach one million Cubans to read and write was the mobilization of 100,000 young people, organized in the Conrado Benítez Brigades, to go to the countryside, where they lived with peasants and workers they were teaching. As a result of this drive, Cuba virtually eliminated illiteracy. During the literacy campaign nine participants, both students and teachers, were murdered by counterrevolutionaries organized, armed, and financed by Washington. Fifty-two percent of the young literacy brigadistas were women.

into the literacy effort, with boys and girls aged ten, eleven, and twelve teaching others, including adults, how to read and write. Women made up over half of the literacy volunteers. And, of course, illiteracy was greater among women than men.

Later on, I also spent time working in the general staff of the Eastern Army with its teaching section, from February 1963 until August 1964. As the one in charge of education within the Eastern Army, I worked on assigning the teachers who were to instruct the rebels in reading, since many of the soldiers had been illiterate.

WATERS: How were women organized in the early years of the revolution? Did you yourself play a part in this?

PUEBLA: Before the revolutionary victory, women were objects—mere bed decorations. After the revolution, this changed. Women began to organize massively working to change the conditions of their lives and to free themselves.

On August 23, 1960, several organizations came together to form the Federation of Cuban Women (FMC). Vilma Espín was president. It joined together in a single organization all the women's organizations that existed at the time.

From the beginning, the Federation worked to incorporate women into the struggle through bringing them into the work force.[2] Because when a woman begins to work outside

2. In 1958, before the revolution triumphed, there were only 194,000 women employed—less than 20 percent of the work force—and 70 percent of these worked as domestic servants. By the early 1990s the figure had risen to 1.4 million, and women were employed in countless sectors that had previously been off limits to women. Women in Cuba currently constitute over 42 percent of the work force. In 1994 the comparable figure in the United States was 46 percent.

"I was 15 when I joined the July 26 Movement in 1956. The situation in Cuba was critical."

COUNCIL OF STATE OFFICE OF HISTORICAL AFFAIRS

Top: Peasant woman and children after having been evicted from their farm by the U.S.-owned Francisco Sugar Co. plantation in Camagüey province.

Bottom: Batista police occupy and sack University of Havana, April 21, 1956; in front with sunglasses is Rafael Salas Cañizares, one of the regime's most notorious murderers. The university remained shut down until the Batista regime fell January 1, 1959.

BOHEMIA

BOHEMIA

BOHEMIA

Top: Demonstration at the University of Havana a few months after March 10, 1952, military coup. The students are bearing a coffin containing the constitution of 1940, giving symbolic burial to the rule of law under the Batista regime.

Bottom: July 31, 1957: police in Santiago de Cuba turn firehose on women protesting the dictatorship's murder of July 26 Movement leader Frank País the day before.

Right: Demonstration in Santiago de Cuba, January 4, 1957, protesting the police murder of 15-year-old William Soler. The sign reads: "Stop the murder of our children. Cuban mothers." At front, in light-colored jacket, is Soler's mother.

"We joined the struggle because of all the abuses, the outrages, the torture, the murders committed by the Batista dictatorship and its henchmen. Just about all the young people in town joined the fight."

BOHEMIA

PHOTOS: GRANMA

Top: Batista army eviction of peasants in the Sierra Maestra. **Bottom:** Rolando Masferrer, pro-Batista businessman and politician who led the death squad known as "Masferrer's Tigers." The photo, from January 1959, was taken as he was leaving the Immigration and Naturalization Service center in McAllen, Texas, after being admitted to the United States. **Facing page, top:** Rebel Army school for peasant children and families, one of more than 400 created in 1958 in the territory of the Second Eastern Front led by Raúl Castro. **Bottom:** workshop for fabrication of arms and ammunition, also in Rebel Army's Second Eastern Front.

"We were fighting for the people and our revolution, while they were defending a dictatorship that was murdering and destroying."

PHOTOS: FUERZAS ARMADAS REVOLUCIONARIAS

PHOTOS: COURTESY TETÉ PUEBLA

This page, top: Members of the Mariana Grajales Women's Platoon in the Liberty Caravan, January 1959. The caravan traveled from Santiago de Cuba to Havana, greeted by an outpouring of popular support in every city and town. Left to right: Teté Puebla, Eloísa Ballester, Lilia Rielo. **Bottom:** Raúl Castro Mercader driving jeep in San Andrés, Holguín, with (left to right) Lilia Rielo, Teté Puebla, and Isabel Rielo, late 1958, after the town was liberated by the Rebel Army.

Facing page, top: Fidel Castro with members of the platoon, October 8, 1958, as they were leaving on a combat mission in the plains. From left to right: Fidel Vargas, Lola Feria, Edemis Tamayo, Teté Puebla, Fidel Castro, Isabel Rielo, Celia Sánchez, Lilia Rielo, Marcelo. **Bottom:** Celia Sánchez (third from left), in Holguín during the Liberty Caravan, with (right to left) Isabel Rielo, Teté Puebla, Lilia Rielo, and two militia members.

“Some men said, ‘How can we give rifles to women when there are so many men who are unarmed?’ . . .

PHOTOS: COURTESY TETÉ PUEBLA

COUNCIL OF STATE OFFICE OF HISTORICAL AFFAIRS

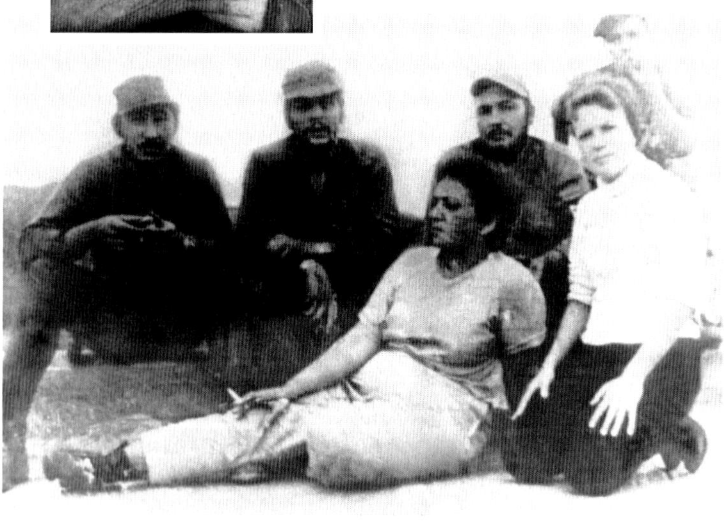

INSTITUTE OF CUBAN HISTORY

Women in the Rebel Army took on many assignments. **Top:** Rebel Army combatants on the march, 1958. Haydée Santamaría, followed by Celia Sánchez and Universo Sánchez. **Center:** Violeta Casals, former television actress who in 1958 became a prominent announcer for Radio Rebelde, the station established by the Rebel Army broadcasting from the Sierras. **Bottom:** Che Guevara, second from left, with Rebel Army courier Lidia Doce (seated). While on a mission in September 1958, Doce was captured and brutally murdered by Batista's forces.

. . . Fidel answered: 'Because they're better soldiers than you are. More disciplined.'"

GRANMA

Above: Members of the Mariana Grajales Platoon after participating in the Battle of Guisa, November 1958: Angelina Antolín, Ada Bella Acosta, Rita García, and Eva Palma together with another combatant.

ANDREW ST. GEORGE COLLECTION/YALE UNIVERSITY LIBRARY

GRANMA

BOHEMIA

Top: Militia unit training in Havana, 1960.

Middle: Founding meeting of the Federation of Cuban Women, August 1960. In the center is Vilma Espín, the organization's president.

Bottom: FACUTE textile mill, Cotorro, Cuba, March 1962.

"Before the revolutionary victory, women were objects, mere bed decorations. After the revolution, women began to organize massively. The revolution sought to incorporate women into the struggle and into the work force."

COURTESY ALICIA IMPERATORI, FMC

GRANMA

Top: Students at the first session of the Ana Betancourt schools for peasant women, 1960. These women came to Havana, where they learned to read and write, and acquired skills such as sewing and embroidering. After graduation, they were given a sewing machine to take home and teach others.

Bottom: Volunteer brigades used government-supplied materials to build homes like these for peasant families, most of whom previously lived in thatch-roofed huts with dirt floors. At right is a sewing machine like those given to graduates of the Ana Betancourt schools.

GRANMA

During 1961 literacy drive, over 100,000 young brigadistas—the majority of them young women—went into the countryside to teach one million Cuban peasants and workers to read and write. **Top left:** brigadistas at December 22, 1961, rally marking the victorious completion of the drive. **Below:** mother and her daughter learning together in San Lorenzo, Sierra Maestra. **Top right:** "Fidel signs first deed," was headline of December 10, 1959, *Revolución* newspaper. Engracia Blet, a female peasant from Baracoa in eastern Cuba, received that deed. Under the agrarian reform some half million members of formerly landless peasant families received plots. Prior to the revolution few women held title to the land they worked.

¡LA REFORMA AGRARIA AVANZA...! ¡LA REFORMA AGRARIA AVANZA...!

FIRMA FIDEL EL PRIMER TITULO

"Comenzamos a dar la tierra a los campesinos por donde mismo empezaron a quitársela los conquistadores a los indios, por Baracoa"

REVOLUCION

2ª EDICION

"Before the revolution the big majority of peasant women were illiterate. Our country was the first in the world to eradicate illiteracy. Women were part of that struggle, young women especially, making up over half of the literacy volunteers."

GRANMA

FLAX HERMES / MILITANT

Top left: Volunteer Cuban workers march on May 1, 1980, in Grenada, during the 1979–83 revolution in that country. **Top right:** Cuban teachers in Ethiopia, during their Sunday combat-readiness training, 1984.

Below: Members of the Women's Antiaircraft Artillery Regiment in Angola, September 1988. In the center, in light blouse, is Vilma Espín.

THIS PHOTO AND BELOW: JUVENTUD REBELDE

"Cuban volunteers went to the Congo, Algeria, Vietnam, Angola, Ethiopia. And women too carried out internationalist missions. In Angola we formed the Women's Antiaircraft Artillery Defense Regiment."

"A country where women and men work and fight side by side is invincible."

Top: Workers at the Heroes of Moncada cigar factory in Havana, 1994.

Bottom: Cuban working people receive regular military training during monthly Defense Day exercises.

Facing page: A woman's company of the Territorial Troop Militia during Defense Day target practice.

ARGIRIS MALAPANIS / MILITANT

GRANMA

GRANMA

MILITANT

"This characteristic of our revolution is called humanity. We identify with all peoples of the world who fight against misery and hunger. If the revolution didn't have this quality, we wouldn't exist."

MARTÍN KOPPEL / MILITANT

GRANMA

Facing page, top: Cuban youth leaders Yanelis Martínez (center) and Javier Dueñas (right) visit site where 19-year old Timothy Thomas was killed by cops, Cincinnati, April 2001. **Facing page, bottom:** Working people of Venezuela poured out of barrios and shantytowns of Caracas and other cities to protest a U.S.-instigated coup against President Hugo Chávez, April 2002.

Top: Cuban and U.S. young people discuss the political struggles they are involved in during Cuba-U.S. Youth Exchange meeting at the School of Social Work, near Havana, July 2001. **Bottom:** Young working people from the countryside and working-class neighborhoods throughout Latin America study medicine, free of charge, at the Latin American School of Medical Sciences in Havana.

"We face a powerful enemy that demands greater unity, steadfastness, and heroism. These times require combatants with a guerrilla spirit, a rebel spirit. Such a spirit exists within our people."

BRIAN TAYLOR / MILITANT

GRANMA

Top: Members of the Revolutionary Armed Forces border guard outside the U.S. naval base at Guantánamo, 1996. **Bottom:** May 1, 2002, demonstration in Havana demands freedom for five Cuban revolutionaries framed up and imprisoned in the United States.

> The Cuban woman, doubly humiliated and relegated to the background by the semicolonial society, needed this organization of her own to represent her specific interests and to work for her broader participation in the economic, political, and social life of the revolution.
>
> Guided by this objective, the Federation of Cuban Women has carried out countless valuable activities in the most varied fields. It has helped to involve over half a million women in production and services; it has mobilized women for many mass tasks such as the country's defense, the literacy campaign, courses to advance their educational level, agricultural work, public health, solidarity, and political studies, whose most important and decisive result has been the remarkable change that has taken place in the political and ideological consciousness of our female population, undoubtedly one of the most outstanding historical victories that the revolution can exhibit today.
>
> FIDEL CASTRO
>
> Report to First Congress of Communist Party of Cuba, December 1975

her home, she organizes her life and she develops. This happened in all stages of the revolution. And among women of all ages and in all occupations.

Before the triumph, many women used to come in from the countryside to work as servants in the homes of the rich. So the federation opened up schools for them. We established the Ana Betancourt schools here in Havana, named after a combatant from the independence war of 1868. Some of the mansions in Miramar, like those in which the women used to work, were turned into schools and dormitories for them.

In the Ana Betancourt schools the women learned to read and write; in addition, they were taught to sew and embroider. When their studies were over, and they graduated in cutting and sewing, Fidel ordered that each one be given a sewing machine to take home. The commitment was they would use it to teach someone else. You'd see these machines in peasants' homes in the mountains and on the plains.

I was involved in helping to recruit the first campesinas for the Ana Betancourt School.

To get those peasant women to come, to get the men to agree wasn't easy. A lot of machismo existed. Some men would say, "Not my daughter" or "Not my wife." And we had to work hard to bring them into the revolutionary process, to convince the men why we had to teach sewing, that it would be a help to their families.

During the final years of the dictatorship there were also many prostitutes. They were brought into the revolution, too. They were given housing because many were from outside Havana and had no homes here. We built schools for them and found them jobs in workplaces.

An especially big effort was made toward women who had worked as prostitutes in Havana. It was true elsewhere too, but the largest concentration had been in Havana. Before the revolution, it was even considered a privilege for these women to prostitute themselves in Havana, because of the greater possibilities for getting out of the country.

These women had taken the road of prostitution because they couldn't find work under capitalism. But the revolution changed that. The Federation of Cuban Women played a role in this, a very important one.

Today no one talks about who was once a prostitute, who was this, that, or the other. And few people know anymore.

Breaking down prejudices

KOPPEL: How did the prejudices against women joining the labor force begin to break down?

PUEBLA: In the Sierra Maestra the work of incorporating women into schools and jobs was easier. Because the peasants had seen us with them there from the beginning. It was harder in other places; you have to keep in mind the low cultural level of the peasants before the revolution, the isolation and lack of access to education.

These prejudices were still strong a full decade after the revolution's victory.

In March 1969, on the order of the commander in chief, I was named director of the Guaicanamar Cattle Plan in Jaruco, in Havana province. He said he was putting me in charge to demonstrate that women could lead as well as men, to show that women could lead an agricultural project, that women could head up any front and carry out any task of the revolution. So Fidel took eight women who were directors of plans—Isabel Rielo among them—to show that women could also lead in agriculture. Part of our job was to get the peasant women there involved in work.

When Fidel took me to the Jaruco zone, the peasants there said they wouldn't work with me. She might be a captain, they said, but she's not working with me. "The commander might have brought you, but I still won't work with women."

But after I'd been there a month, the peasants were working with me. The fact that I worked the same as they did, during the day, the night, Saturdays, Sundays, and so on, gave them confidence, so they understood that I could be a farmer. I had to show that I was their equal, in order to demonstrate that women could do anything.

So women began to join the work in the fields there too. The party, the women's federation, the CDRs,[3] and other organizations all played a role. And we opened over a dozen schools in that zone.

KOPPEL: Was there something special about the Jaruco region?

PUEBLA: This region was dominated by the Jehovah's Witnesses religious sect, and there had been many peasants there who had taken up arms against the revolution, and some even were executed for their crimes. But we knew the peasants there could be won to the revolution, and that was the fundamental task.

That was my assignment until 1978. So I did almost ten years' worth of political work there. That area is now part of my life. In fact, I still dream about the people there. I feel very close to them; they're like family.

Women in defense

WATERS: You spoke earlier of how the Mariana Grajales Platoon was the forerunner of women's role in defense of the Cuban Revolution. How has this developed over the years?

PUEBLA: Women in Cuba have always been on the front line of the struggle. At Moncada we had Yeyé [Haydée

3. The Committees for the Defense of the Revolution (CDR) were organized in 1960 on a block-by-block basis as a mass organization through which the Cuban people could exercise vigilance against counterrevolutionary activity. The CDRs have also organized participation at mass demonstrations and taken part in vaccination and other public health campaigns, civil defense, the fight against petty crime, and other civic tasks.

Santamaría] and Melba [Hernández].[4] With the *Granma* and November 30, we had Celia, Vilma, and many other compañeras. There were many women comrades who were tortured and murdered.

From the beginning there were women in the Revolutionary Armed Forces. First they were simple soldiers, later sergeants. Those of us in the Mariana Grajales Platoon were the first officers. The ones who ended the war with officers' ranks stayed in the armed forces.

Today there's a women's regiment in the Border Guard Battalion at the Guantánamo U.S. naval base in Caimanera,[5] commanded by Lt. Col. Victoria Arrauz Caraballo, who was named by the minister of the armed forces to be second in command of the Border Guard Battalion that guards that territory. There are women in all the military units. They're captains, majors, colonels. Women have also carried out internationalist missions. They went to Angola, to Ethiopia and elsewhere. By the time of the Angola mission, we had formed the Women's Antiaircraft Artillery Defense Regiments. The

4. On July 26, 1953, some 160 revolutionaries under the command of Fidel Castro launched an insurrectionary attack on the Moncada army garrison in Santiago de Cuba together with a simultaneous attack on the garrison in Bayamo, opening the revolutionary armed struggle against the Batista dictatorship. After the attack's failure, Batista's forces massacred more than fifty of the captured revolutionaries. Fidel Castro and twenty-seven others, including Raúl Castro and Juan Almeida, were tried and sentenced to up to fifteen years in prison. They were released on May 15, 1955, after a public defense campaign forced Batista's regime to issue a general amnesty for political prisoners.

5. A reference to the U.S. naval base at Caimanera in Guantánamo Bay in southeastern Cuba, set up shortly after the U.S. military occupation of Cuba in 1898. Since 1959 it has been held against the demand of the Cuban government that it be returned.

members of the regiment assigned to Angola belonged to various combat units.

WATERS: Does the Women's Antiaircraft Regiment still exist in Cuba?

PUEBLA: No. Women are now integrated into all the military units, in antiaircraft, tanks, and every other military specialty. They're ready for any situation. They're prepared to fight.

WATERS: The example of the women's combat units—the Mariana Grajales Platoon, the Women's Antiaircraft Regiments—exemplify the gains of the Cuban Revolution and the leadership's support for women's equality. In the United States we don't demand women's combat units—we're opposed to anything that strengthens the imperialist armed forces!—but we often point out that the formation of such units at different times in the course of the Cuban Revolution demonstrates what Cuba's socialist revolution has meant for women. In the U.S. armed forces there are no female combat units, and very few women in frontline combat posts.

PUEBLA: Here we won this right in the revolutionary war and then it continued in the tank units, in the artillery, in other units. Today there are military schools at the university level. There's the José Martí Military Technical Institute (ITM), which teaches aviation, missiles, computers, communications, and other engineering. There's the Antonio Maceo School in Havana and the José Maceo Military Academy in Santiago de Cuba, where they study all types of weapons, such as tanks, artillery, and infantry weapons, in addition to politics and engineering. There's the *Granma* Naval Academy, where students study both military and civil naval specialties. There's the Baraguá School of Special Forces, the Arístides Estévez School of Counterintelligence, and the Máximo Gómez Higher Academy. Women are present in all of these, both as teachers and as cadets in the various specialties. Women in the military advance to wherever their abilities take them.

This starts with the Camilitos, high school students at the Camilo Cienfuegos Military Schools, named in honor of that magnificent fighter who is loved very much by young people.

MADRID: Are there a lot of young women in the Camilitos?

PUEBLA: Definitely. Every province in Cuba has military vocational schools. In other words, we have military schools throughout the country, in addition to schools for militia members.

The women begin in the tenth grade. They're Camilitas. The schools are for both boys and girls. Before they finish twelfth grade, they choose their next school for continuing their studies, based on the specialty they've chosen. It could be the ITM, where they'll be trained as lawyers or engineers. Or they go to medical school, to become military doctors. And there are scientists and members of other specialties.

KOPPEL: What type of military training do the girls get in school?

PUEBLA: There are military classes in the primary schools as part of the interest circles. In the schools interest circles exist in many areas: chemistry, economics, nursing, nutrition, medicine, the police. And there are military interest circles. I have grandchildren—a ten-year-old, a five-year-old, another who's eight, and another who's twelve—and they get military training as part of the circles they've joined at school. They want to know how to fight if our country is attacked.

KOPPEL: Does everyone learn how to use weapons?

PUEBLA: Yes, there are shooting ranges, and everyone does target practice. Everyone knows how to shoot here, young people among them.

Members of the Association of Combatants of the Cuban

Revolution,[6] are brought in to demonstrate the use of specific weapons to those in the interest circles. Other times active members of the Revolutionary Armed Forces (FAR) go to the schools and show them weapons we in the Combatants Association don't have. And the students in the interest circles sometimes visit military units.

That's why I said everyone in our country—women, men, and children—know what to do if there's a war. Everyone trains. When the alarm sounds, everyone heads to their assigned spot, to their school, wherever they're supposed to go, according to the plan that each family member knows. Each woman in the country knows what she has to do.

One of the things we have is the Day of Defense, which is now held every three months. A given Sunday is designated as a Day of Defense, and people participate in training exercises in defense of the homeland. This includes Production and Defense Brigades, as well as evacuation groups.

On that day I go to my home, where I'm an elected deputy, and I participate with the municipal government in defense exercises. My whole family takes part. I have three children and five grandchildren, the oldest of whom is in eighth grade. One of my duties is to help raise and educate them, with whatever time I have, setting an example for them. The family is something very important for us. Of my three children Laura is a lawyer, Fidel has a degree in international relations, and Raúl is a computer engineer.

6. Organization formed in 1991 of veteran fighters from the Rebel Army, of the clandestine struggle in the cities, Playa Girón, the fight against the counterrevolutionary bands, and Cuba's internationalist missions. Composed of over 300,000 combatants, ACRC members participate in revolutionary tasks and play an active role in relaying the revolution's history and lessons to the younger generations.

During the Day of Defense, my grandchildren participate at school. My daughter is in a production and defense brigade. She's got little children so she can't be in a combat unit. There are other tasks within the revolution, and everyone knows what they're to do.

Military activities are held in parks everywhere. There are centers in residential areas. Weapons are brought over so that women as well as children learn to use them.

Because here we don't know when we might be attacked. We've lived forty-three years in that situation. When we go to bed we don't know how we'll wake up. The people have to be prepared to defend themselves.

WATERS: What about women in active military service?

PUEBLA: Military service is not compulsory for young women, but some women ask to join. It's called Voluntary Military Service. If they have a record of good conduct, they are then eligible for the benefits of Order 18 of the Revolutionary Armed Forces, which entitles them to apply for university admission.

Order 18 of the armed forces permits a recruit with good conduct during their second year of military service to begin taking university preparation courses to get ready for entrance exams in their chosen field. It's based on an individual's performance, on whether the young person is disciplined and capable. Order 18 has become quite common, and is meant to ease the passage from military service into the university, for young people of both sexes and from all social backgrounds. Later, if the person passes the entrance exam, they're admitted as regular students. This program is open to everyone; it's for women as well as men, and of course for blacks as well as whites. In Cuba, beginning in 1959, the revolution eradicated racial discrimination, and this is now set forth in our constitution.

COURTESY TETÉ PUEBLA

Rebel Army officers Teté Puebla and Raúl Castro Mercader leaving the town hall where they were married on March 20, 1960. The band is from the Eastern Army.

WATERS: What are some of the reasons for the different approach toward men and women in military service? What special problems do women confront?

PUEBLA: The revolution has brought enormous progress for women. But we all recognize that whatever the talk of equality, of men sharing household tasks with women, we still have not achieved total equality. They do a few tasks, but when we get home we still have to do or direct everything. It hasn't been easy for women these forty-three years of blockade. All the material shortages have meant greater difficulties for us than for men, for the reasons I've already given.

WATERS: How are these differences reflected in the treatment of women in the FAR? On questions of absenteeism, for example, and disciplinary measures.

PUEBLA: Usually when women are absent it's because of things that men don't go through. Parents have to take care of their children. If a child gets sick, it's almost always the woman who deals with it. Or if the woman is going to have a baby and she needs maternity leave. Men don't go through these things. That's the reason women in the military are treated differently than men.

I've been in the military for forty-six years. As far as I remember, there have been no cases of disciplinary infractions in the armed forces where we've had to give out a long prison sentence to a woman. I don't remember a single case.

No woman has been executed since the revolution triumphed. Despite the fact that there are women here who have committed terrible crimes, such as during the period of the counterrevolutionary bands in the early 1960s. There was one bandit known as "the Girl from Placetas" who had murdered peasants. She even killed her own child. She was surrounded by revolutionary troops and she drowned her own son so he wouldn't cry and get her caught. She murdered men, women, and children. After she was captured and tried, she wasn't executed; she was sentenced to many years in jail instead.

There was another woman called *la coronela,* [the colonel]. Her husband had been a colonel in Batista's army, and she would show up at people's homes and say, as she did once in Bayamo to the mother of the Reyes children, "If you give me 3,000 pesos we won't kill your children." And the peasants sold their cows, they sold everything to raise the money. This woman took all five children of one family and tossed their dead bodies at the family's doorstep.

These were murderers, but in our revolution they weren't executed. Instead they were given lengthy prison terms.

Special Period

WATERS: You mentioned that the shortages created by the U.S. economic war on Cuba have hit women harder than men, especially at home. This has been a particularly weighty factor during the Special Period that Cuba confronted throughout the last decade.[7] How do women confront the daily difficulties that the Special Period has posed?

PUEBLA: If the government has to reduce electrical use during the peak hours in certain places, well, we prepare for it. We monitor the use of electricity. Right now the power supply is stable. But due to the aggression, to the blockade that the U.S. government maintains against our people, we are dependent on uncertain oil imports. There are limits on consumption.

7. The Special Period is the term used in Cuba for the extremely difficult economic conditions the Cuban people have faced since the early 1990s, and the policies the leadership has implemented in face of them to defend the revolution. See glossary, Special Period.

> The presence of women is neither a political question nor a simple struggle for equality, although the struggle for equality is manifested in this and many other forms. It's a necessity, and the potential force represented by women as fighters in defense of the homeland is really extraordinary. This is why it was decided that each regiment of the Territorial Troop Militia in every provincial capital will have a women's battalion and that every municipal battalion will include a women's company. In other words, every province will have its women's battalion and every municipality will have at least one women's company.
>
> I sincerely believe that we're organizing a formidable force, an extraordinary force that will multiply the combat capacity of our Revolutionary Armed Forces and all our people.
>
> FIDEL CASTRO, JANUARY 20, 1981

And we adapt. If we have to bathe before dawn, we do so. We live and get used to it. We leave buckets of water to be able to cook when we get home. So if a blackout hits at any time and we have to wash clothes for the children, we can do it. We've adapted to all those situations. How could we survive otherwise? At the present time, measures have been taken so that the effect on the population is less.

But there's something that needs to be stressed. No school has been closed. No child has ended up in the street. The hospitals remain open. Medicines are provided. Doctors get help in order to do their job.

MADRID: How has this affected women in the FAR? Are there fewer women than before?

PUEBLA: The active-duty forces have been reduced in size. In terms of reductions in the armed forces, however, women have been treated the same as men.

But what are the Cuban armed forces? We're the people in uniform. We're Cuba's sons and daughters. Our armed forces have lived all the pain that the people have. We've been a part of all the work of the revolution.

And we should stress one thing. Even though there are fewer active-duty members of the armed forces today, the Cuban people are fully prepared for a war if it were to be imposed on us.

Depending on the needs of the armed forces at any given point, we have people retiring, too. But even though they're no longer on active duty, if they had to lead a life of combat again, they're ready for it. They know how to handle tanks, how to use cannons and machine guns. They're ready for defense, they're prepared. This is what we call the War of the Entire People.

I can retire today or tomorrow, but I'm ready, whether in my combat unit, or in my political work. I am and will always be a Mariana in combat.

Each woman knows what to do in time of war. I'm not just talking about members of the armed forces, but women on the block. They know where to go, where to take the kids, whether they have to work on a farm, go to a hospital, go to a school, how to protect themselves.

Many acts of aggression have been directed at us during the 43 years of blockade against the Cuban people. But a country where women and men have fought and worked together is invincible. How are they going to defeat our people? How are they going to defeat our revolution?

'The revolution is our reason for being'

WATERS: The U.S. rulers know perfectly well what they would confront if they invaded Cuba.

PUEBLA: That's why they haven't attacked us.

There are counterrevolutionary organizations the U.S. is sponsoring here that want to stir up riots, and engage in other activities. The government doesn't intervene because every block has its Rapid Response Detachment.[1] These groups are under surveillance, and everyone is ready to respond.

They can't do anything because the revolution is ours, it's the people's. It doesn't belong to a little group that wants to come and tell us: "Do as we say." No, this revolution belongs to the people.

There's a popular saying: "The enemy's not taking my street. My city will be defended inch by inch, house by house. We'll die here but they're not going to take our town."

That's why the Association of Combatants is so important. In addition to the CDRs, the FMC, and the party. The Cuban people are ready to defend their homeland.

Like when they killed Pérez Quintosa and others during

1. Formed in 1991 to mobilize community residents to meet any U.S.-encouraged counterrevolutionary actions in Cuba.

an attempted hijacking in Tarará.[2]

Like August 5, when our commander went to the front. The whole people supported him and the thing ended right there, on August 5.[3]

Sometimes we're asked, "Why are you always thinking about war?" We don't like thinking about war, because we don't like war. We like life, happiness, we love people. But they force us to live like this due to a tightening blockade that obligates us to stay on the alert.

Our problems are with the U.S. government and its blockade and all the other attacks. But not with the people of the United States. There's a people-to-people identification.

2. In January 1992 police officer Rolando Pérez Quintosa and three other Cuban security personnel were assaulted in Tarará, a beachfront east of the capital, and murdered by a group of seven attackers who were attempting to hijack a boat in order to leave for the United States. Faced with the revolutionaries' determined resistance, which cost them their lives, the attackers were unable to seize the boat and were forced to flee. All were arrested within hours.

3. On August 5, 1994, a group of some twenty Cubans tried to hijack a boat in Havana harbor to go to Florida. There had been four previous boat hijackings that month, including one a day earlier in which hijackers killed a young Cuban police officer. The August 5 attempted hijacking was repelled by dock workers and the police in Havana.

Later that day a mob of several hundred gathered along the Malecón, Havana's oceanfront boulevard, throwing rocks and bottles at police, hotels, and other targets. Several thousand workers and youth, supporters of the revolution, poured into the streets to respond to the provocation, effectively quelling the riot. They were joined on foot by President Fidel Castro.

Two days later, on August 7, half a million Cubans paid tribute to the slain police officer and demonstrated their support for the revolution in the streets of Havana. Every year since then, August 5 has been celebrated by mass demonstrations and other events.

You could see this in the recent case of the kidnapping of the child Elián [González]. The majority of the people in the United States favored his return to Cuba. With the support of people in the United States and throughout the world, and with the determination of the Cuban people, with those marches by our fighting people, we brought Elián back.[4]

People there want what we want, an end to the blockade. We don't have anything against the people of the United States and they don't have anything against us.

It's the U.S. administrations and those Cubans who are traitors to their country, many of whom ended up in Miami. Among them are people who have committed acts of sabotage, who participated in attempts on Fidel's life, people responsible for the deaths of many Cubans.

Take Jorge Mas Canosa. According to the perpetrators themselves, he gave money to finance the bombing of the Barbados plane.[5] He has been linked to more than forty acts of sabotage committed against the Cuban people. The group he founded has close ties to many in the U.S. government.

4. In November 1999, five-year-old Elián González was found clinging to a raft in the Caribbean after he had been taken by his mother in an illegal departure from Cuba; his mother perished in the shipwreck. Rather than returning him immediately to his father in Cuba, U.S. Immigration authorities brought him to Miami and placed him in the custody of distant relatives, who, with U.S. government complicity, refused to return him to his immediate family in Cuba. In face of almost weekly mass mobilizations by the Cuban people for Elián's return, and majority support within the United States for the boy being returned to his father, in June 2000 the U.S. government was forced to let him return.

5. On October 6, 1976, Cuban counterrevolutionaries set off a bomb on a Cubana Airlines flight from Barbados to Cuba. All seventy-three people aboard were killed.

Who was killed in that plane over Barbados? Some were young people fourteen, sixteen, and seventeen years of age. There was the entire Cuban junior fencing team, which was returning victorious to the country from their competition in the Pan American Games in Caracas. I should mention that we're helping the families of the victims of that act.

The people who committed this crime are the real terrorists.

Yet the ones they find guilty are our compañeros, the five heroic prisoners of the empire: Fernando González, René González, Antonio Guerrero, Gerardo Hernández, and Ramón Labañino.[6] These compañeros are not criminals, they're ordinary working people who were there defending our homeland. They were trying to prevent all those acts of sabotage that are committed against our people. And to prevent acts of terrorism against our people. Three were given life sentences. Yet they're innocent; they simply were trying to save the world from so many deaths.

Meanwhile, the real terrorists go free. People like Posada Carriles. They're setting the stage for freeing him in Panama,

6. In September 1998 the FBI announced with much fanfare that it had discovered a "Cuban spy network" in Florida. In June 2001, five defendants were convicted on charges of "conspiracy to act as an unregistered foreign agent." Three were also convicted of "conspiracy to commit espionage," and one was also convicted of "conspiracy to commit murder." Sentences ranging from 15 years to double life terms plus 15 years were handed down against them. The five imprisoned revolutionaries had accepted assignments to live in the United States and infiltrate counterrevolutionary groups to keep the Cuban government informed about terrorist attacks being planned against Cuba. Inspired by the steadfastness of the five—who each received the title "Hero of the Republic of Cuba"—the Cuban people have mobilized massively to protest their imprisonment and condemn the conditions under which they have been incarcerated.

after he threatened the life of our commander in chief, as well as thousands of Panamanian students.[7]

I can't stop feeling I'm a guerrilla

Waters: It's been forty-six years and you're still on active duty.

Puebla: Right now my assignment continues to be in the Revolutionary Armed Forces Directorate of Attention to combatants and to the families of those who have fallen in defense of the country. I oversee all the things I've talked about, even the schools, of everyone who's suffered in all the battles over the years. I attend to the needs of the families of the combatants of the war of liberation in the mountains and the cities, of the struggle against bandits, of Girón, of internationalist missions. All those who have sacrificed for our country are taken care of.

I'm also a member of the National Executive Committee of the Association of Combatants of the Cuban Revolution led by Commander of the Revolution Juan Almeida. I belong to many work commissions, the Communist Party's ideological commission, for example.

In addition, I'm a deputy to the National Assembly of People's Power, and am a permanent member of its Defense

7. Luis Posada Carriles was one of the organizers of a 1976 bombing of a Cubana Airlines plane over Barbados that killed 73 people. Arrested and convicted for that crime, he served eight years in prison before escaping with the help of bribes provided by the Cuban American National Foundation led by Jorge Mas Canosa, as Posada Carriles himself admitted to the *New York Times* in 1998. In November 2000 he led a plot to assassinate Fidel Castro at a public meeting when the latter was in Panama to attend the Ibero-American Summit. The plot was foiled by Cuban security forces and Posada Carriles was arrested, but the Panamanian government has rejected Cuba's request to extradite him.

GRANMA

The thirteen founding members of the Mariana Grajales Women's Platoon in September 1988, the thirtieth anniversary of the unit's founding.

Commission. We are the people's deputies. The only wage I get is from the FAR.

Forty-six years may sound like a long time, but I don't see myself as a hero, just a regular person. We don't like to talk about what we've done since it's just our daily work and daily lives. We've lived the revolution so intensely that we can't separate it from ourselves. It's our reason for being.

I can't stop feeling I'm a guerrilla. Today we're defending the same ideas of Martí and of the Moncada. But we do so with other, heavier weapons, and we face a powerful enemy that demands greater unity and steadfastness, not to mention heroism. These times require combatants with a guerrilla spirit, a rebel spirit. Such a spirit exists within our people—a people who in the midst of all the difficulties remain loyal to our commander in chief.

So if I were to be born again, I'd do exactly the same as I've done until now.

Being a general of the Revolutionary Armed Forces of Cuba, a military force that has never been a mercenary one, constitutes the pride of our lives. Because every member of the Revolutionary Armed Forces represents all of our dead. The war of liberation cost twenty thousand dead. And others died later.

From the days of the war of liberation up to the present, we work and live for the people. We're a people in uniform.

So I'm proud of being a soldier, of wearing the olive green uniform. And we will defend this uniform to our last breath.

Glossary

Almeida, Juan (1927–2009) – A bricklayer in Havana and a member of the Orthodox Party at the time of Batista's 1952 coup, he was recruited to the movement led by Fidel Castro and participated in the 1953 Moncada attack; sentenced to ten years in prison. Released with the other Moncada prisoners in May 1955 following a national amnesty campaign, he participated in the *Granma* expedition of November–December 1956. In February 1958 he was promoted to commander and later headed the Third Eastern Front. Almeida carried numerous responsibilities since 1959, including head of the air force, vice minister of the Revolutionary Armed Forces, and vice president of the Council of State and Council of Ministers. He was one of three Sierra combatants to receive the title Commander of the Revolution. He was a member of the Communist Party Central Committee and Political Bureau from 1965 until his death. He was the founding president of the Association of Combatants of the Cuban Revolution and a Hero of the Republic of Cuba, the country's highest honor.

Batista, Fulgencio (1901–1973) – Former army sergeant who helped lead a military coup by junior officers in September 1933, in the wake of a popular uprising that had overturned the murderous dictatorship of Gerardo Machado a few weeks earlier. He rose to chief of staff and, in January 1934, organized a second coup that unleashed a reign of repression against workers, peasants, and revolutionary forces. After dominating several governments as army chief of staff, Batista was elected president in 1940. He stepped aside from office in the 1944 elections, but retained a base of support within the army officer corps, living in Florida until 1948. Batista led a coup on March 10, 1952, establishing a brutal military dictatorship that collaborated closely with Washington. He fled to the Dominican Republic with the triumph of the revolution on January 1, 1959.

Betancourt, Ana (1832–1901) – An active participant in Cuba's first war of independence against Spain, 1868–78. She worked as a publicist for the revolutionary cause. She was arrested by Spanish colonial troops and deported, living the remainder of her life in the United States, Jamaica, and then Spain.

Castro Mercader, Raúl (1937–2014) – A member of the July 26 Movement, he joined the Rebel Army in March 1957 as part of the first group of reinforcements sent by Frank País, serving in Columns 1 and 4. In August 1957 he was promoted to captain in Column 4 led by Che Guevara. Served in Angola on internationalist mission. Retired from active duty, he is a brigadier general in the Revolutionary Armed Forces.

Castro Ruz, Fidel (1926–2016) – An active and prominent student leader at the University of Havana from 1945 on, he was the central organizer of Orthodox Party youth after party founding in 1947. He was an Orthodox Party candidate for House of Representatives in the 1952 elections canceled by Batista following the coup in March of that year. In 1953 Castro organized a new revolutionary movement that came to be known as the Centennial Generation, named in honor of the 100th anniversary of José Martí's birth, to carry out the struggle against the Batista dictatorship. He organized and led the July 1953 attack on the Moncada garrison in Santiago de

Cuba. Captured, tried, and sentenced to fifteen years in prison, his courtroom defense speech, History Will Absolve Me, was distributed in tens of thousands of copies across Cuba, becoming the program of the revolutionary movement. Released in 1955 after a mass amnesty campaign, Castro led the founding of the July 26 Revolutionary Movement. He organized the expedition aboard the yacht *Granma* from Mexico in late 1956 and commanded the Rebel Army during the revolutionary war; he became general secretary of the July 26 Movement in May 1958. Following the triumph of the revolution, Castro was Cuba's prime minister from February 1959 to 1976, and was president of the Council of State and Council of Ministers from 1976 to 2006. Commander in chief of the Revolutionary Armed Forces from 1959 to 2006 and first secretary of the Communist Party of Cuba from its founding in 1965 to 2011.

Castro Ruz, Raúl (1931–) – An organizer of University of Havana student protests against the Batista dictatorship, he joined in the 1953 Moncada attack and was sentenced to thirteen years in prison. He was released in May 1955 following a national amnesty campaign. A founding member of the July 26 Movement, he was a participant in the 1956 *Granma* expedition and one of the initial cadres of the Rebel Army. In February 1958 he was promoted to commander and headed the Second Eastern Front. He was minister of the Revolutionary Armed Forces (FAR) from 1959 to 2008 and is General of the Army in the FAR. He was vice premier from 1959 until 1976, first vice president of the Council of State and Council of Ministers from 1976 until 2008, and has been president of the Council of State and Ministers from 2008 to 2018. A founding member of the Communist Party of Cuba. He was its second secretary from 1965 to 2008, first secretary since 2008, and a member of the Political Bureau. He holds the title Hero of the Republic of Cuba.

Cienfuegos, Camilo (1932–1959) – Active opponent of the 1952 Batista coup, Cienfuegos lived in the U.S. in 1953–54, working in garment shops and restaurants in New York, San Francisco, and Chicago before being arrested and deported by U.S. immigration cops. In 1956 he went to Mexico to enlist in the armed struggle against Batista. A *Granma* expeditionary, he became a captain in Che Guevara's Rebel Army column in late 1957. He was promoted to commander in 1958 and from August to October 1958 led the "Antonio Maceo" Column 2 westward on an invasion from the Sierra Maestra en route to Pinar del Río. He operated in northern Las Villas until the end of the war and became Rebel Army chief of staff in January 1959. He was killed when his plane was lost at sea while returning from Camagüey to Havana on October 28, 1959.

Cintra Frías, Leopoldo (Polo) (1941–) – A native of Yara, he joined the Rebel Army in November 1957, finishing the war with the rank of lieutenant. He volunteered for internationalist missions in Angola and Ethiopia in the 1970s and headed Cuba's military mission in Angola 1983–86 and 1989. A Hero of the Republic of Cuba, he is a division general of the FAR and a member of the Political Bureau of the Communist Party of Cuba.

Communist Party of Cuba – In 1961, following a process of differentiation and clarification as the revolution deepened, the July 26 Movement initiated a fusion with the Popular Socialist Party and the Revolutionary Directorate to form the Integrated Revolutionary Organizations (ORI). In 1963 it became the United Party of the Socialist Revolution; and in October 1965 the Communist Party of Cuba, with Fidel Castro as first secretary of its Central Committee.

del Valle, Sergio (1927–2007) – Joined Rebel Army in the Sierra Maestra in 1957 as combatant and physician, promoted to captain in the column led by Che Guevara. In 1958 he served as second in command of Camilo Cienfuegos's column. He was head of the army general staff in 1960s, then minister of interior and of public health. A member of the Communist Party Central Committee from 1965 until his death and of the Political Bureau 1965–86. He was a division general in the Cuban army. In 2001 he received the title Hero of the Republic of Cuba.

Durán Batista, Carlos – Captain in the army of the Batista dictatorship during the revolutionary war, he headed a military unit in Las Vegas de Jibacoa in the Sierra Maestra.

Espín, Vilma (1930–2007) – A member of Revolutionary National Action led by Frank País in Santiago de Cuba that joined in formation of July 26 Movement in 1955. She was a participant in the Santiago uprising of November 30, 1956. She later served as July 26 Movement coordinator in Oriente province. She joined the Rebel Army in July 1958, serving in Second Eastern Front. She was president of the Federation of Cuban Women from 1960 until her death, a member of the Communist Party Central Committee since 1965, and a member of its Political Bureau 1980–91. She was a member of Council of State from 1976 until her death. In 2001 she received the title Heroine of the Republic of Cuba.

Federation of Cuban Women (FMC) – Founded August 23, 1960, with Rebel Army combatant Vilma Espín as its president, it united prorevolutionary women's organizations. Championing the fight for women's equality, the FMC worked to integrate women into the revolution's tasks and the labor force.

Ferrer Benítez, Norma (1941–) – Born in Yara, she joined the Rebel Army and served in Column 1. A founding member of the Mariana Grajales Women's Platoon.

Figueroa, Juan Ramón (Turtó) – Rebel Army combatant from Yara, he served in the First and Second Fronts. He was killed in an accident.

FMC. See Federation of Cuban Women.

Frías, Ángel (1940–1969) – A member of the Rebel Army in Column 1, he became part of Column 8 led by Che Guevara, which in 1958 carried out the westward invasion toward Las Villas province.

Frías, Ciro (1928–1958) – A peasant from the Sierra Maestra, he joined the Rebel Army in January 1957. A member of Column 1, and later a captain in Column 18 in the Second Eastern Front, under the command of Raúl Castro. He was killed April 10, 1958, and was posthumously promoted to commander.

Gómez Ochoa, Delio (1929–) – Rebel Army fighter. After the April 1958 general strike attempt, he became national action coordinator of July 26 Movement, based in Havana. He became commander of Rebel Column 32 and of the Fourth Eastern Front October 1958. After the revolution's victory, he led armed expedition to Dominican Republic in June 1959 by Dominican and Cuban volunteers; captured and later released. He subsequently had responsibilities in the agricultural sector of economy.

González, Fernando (1963–) – One of five Cuban revolutionaries jailed in U.S. after being framed up and convicted in 2001 of "conspiracy to act as an unregistered foreign agent." A member of the Union of Young Communists (UJC), in 1987 he graduated from the Raúl Roa García Higher Institute of International Relations. In 1987–89 he participated in the Cuban military mission in Angola. In the mid-1990s he volunteered for an internationalist mission to live in the United States and develop ties to the Cuban counterrevolutionary groups based there in order to keep the Cuban government informed of operations being planned against Cuba. Arrested in 1998 and sentenced to 19 years in prison, he was released in 2014.

González, René (1956–) – One of five Cuban revolutionaries jailed in U.S. after being framed up and convicted in 2001 of "conspiracy to act as an unregistered foreign agent." He was born in Chicago of parents active in the July 26 Movement. His family returned to Cuba in 1961. A member of the Union of Young Communists, he served in the Cuban military mission in Angola in the late 1980s. Trained as a pilot, he subsequently worked as a flight instructor. In the mid-1990s he volunteered for an internationalist mission to live in the United States and develop ties to the Cuban counterrevolutionary groups based there in order to keep the Cuban government informed of operations being planned against Cuba. Arrested in 1998 and sentenced to 15 years in prison, he was released in 2011.

Grajales, Mariana (1808–1893) – From a poor family, she was an ardent supporter of Cuba's independence. When the war against Spanish colonialism began in 1868, she encouraged all her sons to enlist. Her husband and five sons were killed in the independence struggle. One of her sons was Lieutenant General Antonio Maceo, known as the Bronze Titan, a leader of Cuba's independence wars noted for his courage and heroism.

Granma – The yacht that carried eighty-two revolutionary fighters, including Fidel Castro, Raúl Castro, Ernesto Che Guevara, Camilo Cienfuegos, and Juan Almeida from Tuxpan, Mexico, to Cuba to initiate the revolutionary war against the brutal U.S.-backed regime of Fulgencio Batista. The expeditionaries landed in southeast Cuba on December 2, 1956. *Granma* has been the name of the daily newspaper of the Communist Party of Cuba since 1965. To coincide with the *Granma* landing, the July 26 Movement had planned an uprising in Oriente province. Centered in Santiago de Cuba, the uprising took place November 30, 1956, led by Frank País. Together with the *Granma* landing, it marked the opening of Cuba's revolutionary war.

Guerra, Orestes (1932–) – A native of Yara, he joined the Rebel Army in 1957, serving in columns under the command of Fidel Castro, Che Guevara, and Camilo Cienfuegos and finishing the war as a captain. He is a brigadier general of the FAR, retired.

Guerrero, Antonio (1958–) – One of five Cuban revolutionaries jailed in U.S. after being framed up and convicted in 2001 of "conspiracy to commit espionage" and "conspiracy to act as an unregistered foreign agent." Born in Miami, he returned with his family to Cuba in the first days of January 1959. A high school student leader and member of the Union of Young Communists, he won a scholarship to study in the Soviet Union to be an airport construction engineer. A member of the Communist Party of Cuba, in the mid-1990s he volunteered for an internationalist mission to live in the United States and develop ties to the Cuban counterrevolutionary groups based there in order to keep the Cuban government informed of operations being planned against Cuba. Arrested in 1998 and sentenced to life plus 10 years, he was released in 2014.

Guevara, Ernesto Che (1928–1967) – Argentine-born leader of the Cuban Revolution. A participant in the *Granma* expedition, he was the first Rebel Army combatant to be promoted to the rank of commander during Cuba's revolutionary war. In late 1958 he united various revolutionary forces in central Cuba under his command and led them in the capture of Santa Clara, the island's third most important city. Following the 1959 triumph, in addition to his military tasks, Guevara held a number of positions and responsibilities in the revolutionary government including head of the National Bank and minister of industry; he often represented the revolutionary leadership at international events. In April 1965 he led the Cuban column that fought for seven months alongside anti-imperialist forces in the Congo. In late 1966 he led a vanguard detachment of internationalist volunteers to Bolivia. Wounded and captured by the Bolivian army in a CIA-organized operation on October 8, 1967, he was murdered the following day.

Hernández, Gerardo (1965–) – One of five Cuban revolutionaries jailed in U.S. after being framed up and convicted in 2001 of "conspiracy to commit espionage," "conspiracy to act as an unregistered foreign agent," and "conspiracy to commit murder." A member of the Union of Young Communists, he served in the Cuban military mission in Angola, heading a scouting platoon in a tank brigade. He participated in 54 combat missions before completing his tour in 1990. In the mid-1990s he volunteered for an internationalist mission to live in the United States and develop ties to the Cuban counterrevolutionary groups based there in order to keep the Cuban government informed of operations being planned against Cuba. Arrested in 1998 and sentenced to two life sentences plus 15 years, he was released in 2014.

Hernández, Melba (1921–2014) – She joined the revolutionary movement led by Fidel Castro in 1952 and was one of two women to participate in the Moncada attack of July 26, 1953, serving seven months in prison. When the July 26 Movement was founded in June 1955, she became a member of its National Directorate. Returning to Cuba from Mexico after the *Granma* landing, she carried out intensive underground activity and later joined the Rebel Army in the Third Eastern Front. After 1959 she held a number of leadership and diplomatic positions. She was founder and president of the Committee in Solidarity with Vietnam and the Peoples of

Indochina, vice president of the Anti-Imperialist Tribunal of Our America, a member of the Central Committee of the Communist Party, and director of its Center for Asian Studies. In 2001 she received the title Heroine of the Republic of Cuba.

Herrera, Osvaldo (d. 1958) – Rebel Army captain who served as adjutant to Commander Camilo Cienfuegos in 1958. In June 1958 he was sent to Holguín to reorganize the leadership of the July 26 Movement there. After being taken prisoner by the dictatorship, he committed suicide rather than give his torturers any information.

Iglesias, Joel (1941–2011) – Born into a peasant family on the outskirts of Santiago de Cuba, he joined the Rebel Army in 1957, serving in Columns 4 and 8 under Che Guevara; he was promoted to commander at the end of the revolutionary war. He became the first president of the Association of Rebel Youth, initiated by the Rebel Army Department of Instruction, in 1960, and general secretary of the Union of Young Communists in 1962. He was a member of the Communist Party Central Committee 1965–75.

July 26 Revolutionary Movement – Founded June 1955 by Fidel Castro and other veterans of the attack on the Moncada garrison, along with youth activists from the left wing of the Orthodox Party and other forces, including the National Revolutionary Action led by Frank País in Santiago and veterans of the Revolutionary National Movement such as Armando Hart and Faustino Pérez in Havana. The July 26 Movement separated from the Orthodox Party in March 1956. During the revolutionary war it was composed of the Rebel Army in the mountains *(Sierra)* and the urban underground network *(Llano)*. Fidel Castro became general secretary of the movement in May 1958. It began publishing *Revolución* clandestinely during the revolutionary war. Following the victory the July 26 Movement initiated a process of fusion with the Popular Socialist Party and Revolutionary Directorate and in 1961 they formed the Integrated Revolutionary Organizations (ORI), which subsequently became the United Party of the Socialist Revolution (PURS), and after 1965 the Communist Party of Cuba.

Kindelán, Rolando (1928–2016) – A brigadier general in the Revolutionary Armed Forces. A farm worker from Oriente province, he joined the Rebel Army in June 1957, later becoming a member of Camilo Cienfuegos's column. In 1959 he was named military leader on the Isle of Pines. In 1962 he participated in the struggle against counterrevolutionary bandits. Beginning in 1965 he was second in command, and later commander, of a column of Cuban internationalist combatants based in the Congo-Brazzaville. A member of the Communist Party of Cuba Central Committee, 1965–86. He was president of the Association of Combatants of the Cuban Revolution in the city of Havana.

Labañino, Ramón (1963–) – One of five Cuban revolutionaries jailed in U.S. after being framed up and convicted in 2001 of "conspiracy to commit espionage" and "conspiracy to act as an unregistered foreign agent." A member of the Union of Young Communists who graduated with a degree in economics in 1986, in the mid-1990s he volunteered for an internationalist mission to live in the United States and develop ties to the Cuban counterrevolutionary groups based there in order to keep the Cuban government informed of operations being planned against Cuba. Arrested in 1998 and sentenced to life plus 18 years, he was released in 2014.

Lastre, Manuel (1941–) – Born in Yara, he became a combatant in the Rebel Army and a member of Column 2 under Camilo Cienfuegos that carried out the invasion of Las Villas province in 1958. Currently a brigadier general.

Lorente, Miguel (1937–) – A native of Manzanillo, he joined the Rebel Army in the Sierra Maestra and rose to the rank of lieutenant in Camilo Cienfuegos's column. He took part in internationalist missions in Ethiopia, in the battle of the Ogaden, and in Angola, where he fought in the Cuito Cuanavale campaign in 1988. A brigadier general of the FAR, he retired from active service in 1999.

Lucha Contra Bandidos. See Struggle against bandits

Maceo, Antonio (1845–1896) – Prominent military leader and strategist in Cuba's wars of independence from Spain in the nineteenth century. He was a leader of the 1895–96 westward march from Oriente that culminated in the invasion of Pinar del Río province. He became a symbol of revolutionary intransigence in 1878, at the conclusion of Cuba's first independence war, when he refused to put down his arms against the colonial regime, issuing what became known as the Baraguá Protest. Known in Cuba as the Bronze Titan, he was killed in battle December 7, 1896.

Martí, José (1853–1895) – A noted revolutionary, poet, writer, speaker, and journalist, he is Cuba's national hero. He founded the Cuban Revolutionary Party in 1892 to fight Spanish colonial rule and oppose U.S. designs on Cuba. He organized and planned the 1895 independence war and was killed in battle at Dos Ríos in Oriente province. His revolutionary anti-imperialist program is part of the internationalist traditions and political heritage of the Cuban Revolution.

Martínez Páez, Julio (1908–1999) – Rebel Army commander, he was a combatant and doctor. After the revolution's triumph, he served as minister of public health. A prominent scientist and internationally recognized orthopedic surgeon, he was director of the Fructuoso Rodríguez Orthopedic Hospital.

Mas Canosa, Jorge (1939–1997) – An opponent of the Cuban Revolution, he emigrated to the U.S. in 1960, becoming a wealthy capitalist. The founder and president, from 1981 until his death, of the Cuban American National Foundation, which helped support and fund counterrevolutionary terrorist activities.

Masferrer, Rolando (1914–1975) – A pro-Batista senator and wealthy bourgeois politician. In the 1950s he organized and led a private paramilitary squad of some 2,000 torturers, assassins, and extortionists known as the "Tigers," which worked closely with the dictatorship's army. During Cuba's revolutionary war, the *masferrerista* gangs functioned as death squads, torturing and murdering hundreds, if not thousands, of the regime's opponents. Their principal source of income was from gambling, prostitution, and extortion.

In the 1930s Masferrer had been a member of the Cuban Communist Party (which took the name Popular Socialist Party in 1944) and fought as a volunteer in the Spanish civil war, leaving the party in 1945. He fled Cuba December 31, 1958. Masferrer was killed by a car bomb in Miami in a gangland hit sixteen years later.

Mojena, Omar Iser – Combatant of Rebel Army Column 1 and a founder of the Fourth Front.

Oñate, Alejandro "Cantinflas" (1936–) – Rebel Army combatant. He was promoted to lieutenant and served in Camilo Cienfuegos's Column 2 that carried out westward invasion of central provinces.

Palomares, Pastor (1939–1957) – Joined the Rebel Army April 20, 1957. He was killed in the battle of Palma Mocha August 20, 1957.

Paz, Ramón (1924–1958) – A member of July 26 Movement, he joined the Rebel Army and served as a combatant in Column 1. He was killed in battle July 28, 1958.

Pérez, Faustino (1920–1992) – Active in revolutionary politics at University of Havana before 1952. Following Batista's coup, he became a leader of Revolutionary National Movement together with Armando Hart, most of whose members took part in forming the July 26 Movement. A member of the *Granma* expedition, he headed July 26 Movement urban underground in Havana until April 1958. He then returned to the Sierra Maestra and became a commander. A member of Communist Party Central Committee from 1965 until his death.

Pérez Chávez, Flor (1939–) – Born in Yara, she joined the Rebel Army and became a member of Column 1. A founder of the Mariana Grajales Women's Platoon, she was wounded in the battle of Maffo. She reached the rank of lieutenant.

Playa Girón – On April 17, 1961, an expeditionary force of 1,500 Cuban mercenaries—organized, financed, and deployed by Washington—invaded Cuba at the Bay of Pigs on the southern coast. The counterrevolutionaries aimed to spark an antigovernment uprising while holding a beachhead on Cuban territory long enough to install a provisional government already formed in the United States that would appeal for Washington's support and for direct military intervention. In less than seventy-two hours of intense combat, however, the mercenaries were defeated by Cuba's militias, Revolutionary Armed Forces, Revolutionary Air Force, and Revolutionary National Police. On April 19 the remaining invaders were captured at Playa Girón (Girón Beach), which is the name Cubans use to designate the battle.

Posada Carriles, Luis (1928–2018) – A member of Brigade 2506 that attacked Cuba at the Bay of Pigs in 1961, the invasion was defeated before his unit could land. Trained by the Central Intelligence Agency over four decades, he was linked to numerous sabotage and assassination plots that have taken a high human and economic toll. He was accused of masterminding the 1976 bombing of a Cuban airliner that killed

73 people. In 2000 he was arrested in Panama for a series of bombing attacks.

Quesada, Flavio – A founder of the Rebel Army's Fourth Front, together with Delio Gómez Ochoa. Currently a lieutenant colonel in the Revolutionary Armed Forces.

Radio Rebelde – Rebel Army radio station that began broadcasting February 24, 1958, from Sierra Maestra. During the later months of the war, its transmissions were beamed to Venezuela for rebroadcast to Cuba. It played an important role in disseminating the truth about political and military developments during the revolutionary war.

Redondo, Ciro (1931–1957) – A member of Orthodox Youth, he was won to the revolutionary movement led by Fidel Castro and participated in the 1953 Moncada attack. He was captured, tried, and sentenced to 10 years in prison, but was released in May 1955 following the national amnesty campaign. A *Granma* expeditionary, he became a captain in Rebel Army, serving in Guevara's column. He was killed in battle November 29, 1957; posthumously promoted to commander.

Rielo, Isabel (1940–1989) – Head of the Mariana Grajales Platoon formed in September 1958. A lieutenant in the Rebel Army at the end of the war. Promoted to captain in 1960, she worked in the medical corps, the General Staff, and the Military Technical Institute. She later was assigned to head the Turibacoa Vegetable Plan.

Rielo, Lilia – Born in Santiago de Cuba, she joined Rebel Army Column 1 and became a founding member of the Mariana Grajales Women's Platoon. Retired with the rank of major in the Ministry of the Interior.

Sánchez, Celia (1920–1980) – Born in Manzanillo, near the Sierra Maestra mountains of eastern Cuba, she was a founding member of the Orthodox Party in 1947 and of its youth. She became a leader of the amnesty campaign in Oriente province for the Moncada prisoners. In 1955 she was a founding member of the July 26 Movement, and became its central organizer in Manzanillo. She organized the urban supply and recruitment network for the Rebel Army, and was the first woman to become a combatant in the Rebel Army, serving on its general command beginning October 1957. At her death she was a member of the Communist Party Central Committee and secretary of the Council of State and Council of Ministers.

Sánchez Mosquera, Ángel – A lieutenant in Batista's army notorious for acts of brutality against peasants, he ended the war as a colonel. He escaped Cuba January 1, 1959.

Santamaría, Haydée "Yeyé" (1922–1980) – A participant in the 1953 Moncada attack, in which her brother Abel was captured and brutally murdered, she was imprisoned for seven months. A founder of the July 26 Movement and member of its National Directorate, she helped organize the November 30, 1956, uprising in Santiago de Cuba. During the revolutionary war she carried out numerous underground and international tasks, later becoming a Rebel Army combatant in Column 1 until ordered abroad to carry out various missions among Cubans in exile. She was founder and director of Casa de las Américas from 1959 until her death, and was a member of the Communist Party Central Committee 1965–80.

Sosa, Merob (b. 1920) – Notorious officer of the dictatorship's army in the Sierra Maestra for his crimes and abuses against the peasants and rural population, he graduated from the U.S. Army's School of the Americas in 1956.

Special Period – The term used in Cuba for the extremely difficult economic conditions the Cuban people faced from the early 1990s on, and the policies implemented in face of them to defend the revolution. With the disintegration of the regimes of Eastern Europe and the Soviet Union that previously accounted for 85 percent of Cuba's foreign trade, the island was brutally thrust back into the world capitalist market from which it had been partially sheltered for more than 25 years. The sudden and unilateral break in trading patterns—which took place as the world capitalist crisis intensified, and were exacerbated by the heightened economic warfare organized by Washington—led to the most severe economic crisis in Cuba since 1959. In 1993 and 1994 a number of measures were adopted to address the worsening economic conditions. Even though shortages of food and other essentials remained, by 1996, through the efforts of Cuban working people, inflation was brought under control, and a recovery began.

Struggle against bandits – From 1959 until 1965 the Cuban Revolution waged a battle against CIA-armed and -financed counterrevolutionary bands centered mainly in the Escambray mountains of central Cuba. During these opening years of the revolution, there were at one time or another 299 bands with 4,000 members that carried out assassinations, sabotage, and other terrorist actions. They were defeated largely through the mobilization of peasants and workers from the affected areas themselves. A specialized unit of the Revolutionary Armed Forces—Lucha Contra Bandidos (LCB)—was created to wage the battle.

Suñol, Eddy (1925–1971) – A member of the July 26 Movement in Santiago de Cuba, he joined the Rebel Army in 1957. In 1958 he became head of Column 14 of the Rebel Army's Fourth Front. He finished the revolutionary war with the rank of commander.

Terry, Santiago (1930–1986) – Rebel Army combatant in the Sierra Maestra. He was one of the leaders of the Cuban contingent in the Congo in 1965 and was a colonel in the Revolutionary Armed Forces at the time of his death.

Verdecia, Eugenia (1936–1979) – Born in Yara, she joined the Rebel Army and became a member of Column 1. She ended the war in the Third Front in the municipality of Bartolomé Masó.

Villegas, Harry (Pombo) (1940–2019) – A native of Yara, in Oriente province, he joined the Rebel Army in 1957 and became a member of Che Guevara's personal escort in Columns 4 and 8. He served with Guevara in the Congo, where Che gave him the nom-de-guerre "Pombo," and later in Bolivia, where he was a member of the general staff of the guerrilla movement. After Guevara was killed in October 1967, Villegas commanded the group of surviving combatants that eluded the encirclement jointly organized by the Bolivian army and U.S. military forces, returning to Cuba in March 1968. He served three tours of duty in Angola in the 1970s and 1980s. He was a brigadier general (retired) in the Revolutionary Armed Forces, a member of the Central Committee of the Communist Party, and a deputy in the Cuban National Assembly. He was also executive vice president of the National Directorate of the Association of Combatants of the Cuban Revolution and headed its Secretariat of Patriotic-Military and Internationalist Work. In 1995 he received the title Hero of the Republic of Cuba.

Index

ALSO FROM PATHFINDER

Women in Cuba: The Making of a Revolution Within the Revolution

VILMA ESPÍN
ASELA DE LOS SANTOS
YOLANDA FERRER

The integration of women in the ranks and leadership of the Cuban Revolution was intertwined with the proletarian course led by Fidel Castro from the start. This is the story of that revolution and how it transformed the women and men who made it. $17. Also in Spanish, Farsi, Greek.

Women and the Cuban Revolution

Speeches and Documents by Fidel Castro, Vilma Espín, and others

The victory of the Cuban Revolution, said Fidel Castro in 1966, "has meant a double liberation" for women, "who were discriminated against not only as workers but also as women." Includes the 1975 Family Code, documents of Cuba's Communist Party, and speeches by party leaders. $15

Women's Liberation and the African Freedom Struggle

THOMAS SANKARA

"There is no true social revolution without the liberation of women," explains the leader of the 1983–87 revolution in the West African country of Burkina Faso. $5. Also in Spanish, French, Farsi, Arabic.

CUBA'S SOCIALIST REVOLUTION

New!

Revolution and the Road to Peace in Colombia

The Example of the Cuban Revolution

FIDEL CASTRO

"No crime can be committed in the name of revolution," Fidel Castro declares, drawing from the example set by working people of Cuba as they took state power out of the hands of its capitalist rulers. In 2008, as part of efforts to end six decades of armed conflict in Colombia, he shared the exemplary record of Cuba's revolutionary struggle with the Revolutionary Armed Forces of Colombia (FARC) and the world. $10. Also in Spanish and French.

In Defense of Socialism

Four Speeches on the 30th Anniversary of the Cuban Revolution

FIDEL CASTRO

Not only is social progress possible when freed from capitalism's exploitative relations, the Cuban leader says, but socialism is humanity's only way forward. Castro also describes the decisive place of volunteer Cuban fighters in defeating the invading forces of South Africa's apartheid regime. $12. Also in Greek.

Cuba and Angola: The War for Freedom

HARRY VILLEGAS ("POMBO")

The story of Cuba's unparalleled contribution to the fight to free Africa from the scourge of apartheid. And how, in the doing, Cuba's socialist revolution was strengthened. $10. Also in Spanish, Farsi, Greek.

New!

Cuba and the Independence War in Guinea-Bissau and Cape Verde

The Fall of the Last Colonial Empire in Africa

VÍCTOR DREKE

In 1974–75 the people of two West African countries, Guinea-Bissau and Cape Verde, put an end to 500 years of Portuguese colonial exploitation. Led by a popular movement forged by Amílcar Cabral, their struggle triggered the collapse of Portugal's entire colonial empire and brought down the 40-year fascist dictatorship in Portugal itself. Víctor Dreke's firsthand account brings to life this decisive victory. $12. Also in Spanish.

Che Guevara on Economics and Politics in the Transition to Socialism

CARLOS TABLADA

It's essential for working people to win state power, said Ernesto Che Guevara. "Then there's the second stage, maybe more difficult than the first"—the transition from dog-eat-dog capitalism to socialism. Includes Fidel Castro's 1987 speech "Che's Ideas Are Absolutely Relevant Today." New edition with substantially expanded selections from Guevara's writings. $17. Also in Spanish.

Our History Is Still Being Written

The Story of Three Chinese Cuban Generals in the Cuban Revolution

ARMANDO CHOY, GUSTAVO CHUI
MOISÉS SÍO WONG, MARY-ALICE WATERS

"What was the key measure to uproot discrimination against Chinese and blacks in Cuba? It was the socialist revolution itself." New edition sheds light on Chinese Cubans' involvement in Cuba's internationalist course, including in Africa and Latin America. $15. Also in Spanish, French, Farsi, Greek, Chinese.

The Coming American Revolution

Cuba and the Coming American Revolution

JACK BARNES

This is a book about the example set by the Cuban people that socialist revolution is not only necessary—it can be made. A book about the struggles of workers and other exploited producers in the imperialist heartland, and the youth attracted to them. About the class struggle in the US, where the revolutionary capacities of working people are as utterly discounted by the ruling powers as were those of the Cuban toilers. $10. Also in Spanish, French, Farsi.

The Low Point of Labor Resistance Is Behind Us

The Socialist Workers Party Looks Forward

JACK BARNES
MARY-ALICE WATERS
STEVE CLARK

The global order imposed by Washington is shattering. A long retreat by the working class and unions has come to an end. The bosses and their government are stepping up attacks on our wages, conditions, and constitutional rights. This book highlights opportunities for building a mass proletarian party able to lead the struggle to end capitalist rule, opening a socialist future for humanity. $10. Also in Spanish, French, Greek.

THE WORKING CLASS AND THE FIGHT AGAINST JEW-HATRED

The Fight Against Jew-Hatred and Pogroms in the Imperialist Epoch

Stakes for the International Working Class

V.I. LENIN, LEON TROTSKY
FARRELL DOBBS, JAMES P. CANNON
JACK BARNES, DAVE PRINCE

Jew-hatred and pogroms—such as Hamas carried out on October 7, 2023—are part of the social convulsions and wars of the imperialist epoch. The authors explain why fighting Jew-hatred is decisive to the working class and oppressed nations of the world—and *what is to be done to end it*. $10. Also in Spanish, French, Greek.

Imperialism's March Toward Fascism and War

JACK BARNES

"There will be new Hitlers, new Mussolinis. That is inevitable. What is not inevitable is that they will triumph. The working-class vanguard will organize our class to fight back against the devastating toll we are made to pay for the capitalist crisis. The future of humanity will be decided in the contest between these contending class forces." In *New International* no. 10. $14. Also in Spanish, French, Farsi, Greek.

The Jewish Question

A Marxist Interpretation

ABRAM LEON

The battle against reactionary forces aiming to exterminate the Jews remains central to world politics, as shown by the genocidal October 2023 pogrom in Israel. Why is Jew-hatred still raising its ugly head? What are its class roots? Why, as Abram Leon explains, is there no solution "independent of the world proletarian revolution"? Revised translation, new introduction, 40 pages of illustrations and maps. $17. Also in Spanish, French, Greek.

CAPITALIST CRISIS AND THE FIGHT FOR WORKERS POWER

Malcolm X, Black Liberation, and the Road to Workers Power

JACK BARNES

"The conquest of state power by a class-conscious vanguard of the working class is the mightiest weapon possible in the fight against Black oppression, the subjugation of women, Jew-hatred, and every form of human degradation inherited from class society." $20. Also in Spanish, French, Farsi, Arabic, Greek.

Are They Rich Because They're Smart?

Class, Privilege, and Learning Under Capitalism

JACK BARNES

In battles forced on us by the capitalists, workers will begin to transform our attitudes toward life, work, and each other. We'll discover our worth, denied by the rulers and upper middle classes who insist they're rich because they're smart. We'll learn in struggle what we're capable of becoming. $10. Also in Spanish, French, Farsi, Arabic, Greek.

Is Socialist Revolution in the US Possible?

A Necessary Debate Among Working People

MARY-ALICE WATERS

Fighting for a society only working people can create, it is our own capacities we will discover. And we will answer the question posed here with a resounding "Yes." Revolution is possible but not inevitable. That depends on us. $7. Also in Spanish, French, Farsi.

Opening Guns of World War III: Washington's Assault on Iraq

JACK BARNES

The murderous assault on Iraq in 1990–91 heralded increasingly sharp conflicts among imperialist powers, growing instability of capitalism, and more wars. Also includes:

1945: When US Troops Said 'No!'
by Mary-Alice Waters
Lessons from the Iran-Iraq War
by Samad Sharif

In *New International* no. 7. $14. Also in Spanish, French, Farsi.

Capitalism's Long Hot Winter Has Begun

JACK BARNES

Today's global capitalist crisis is but the opening stage of decades of economic, financial, and social convulsions and class battles. Class-conscious workers confront this historic turning point for imperialism with confidence, Jack Barnes writes, drawing satisfaction from being "in their face" as we chart a revolutionary course to take power. In *New International* no. 12. $14. Also in Spanish, French, Farsi, Arabic, Greek.

The Clintons' Anti-Working-Class Record

Why Washington Fears Working People

JACK BARNES

What working people need to know about the profit-driven course of Democrats and Republicans alike over the last three decades. And the political awakening of workers seeking to understand and resist the capitalist rulers' assaults. $10. Also in Spanish, French, Farsi, Greek.

COMMUNIST PROGRAM AND FORGING PROLETARIAN PARTIES

The Teamster Series

FARRELL DOBBS

Four books on the 1930s strikes, organizing drives, and political campaigns that transformed the Teamsters into a militant industrial union movement. Written by the organizer of these battles and leader of the Socialist Workers Party. A tool for workers seeking to use union power and advance the fight for a party of labor. $16 each, series $50. Also in Spanish. *Teamster Rebellion* is also available in French, Farsi, Greek.

The Turn to Industry

Forging a Proletarian Party

JACK BARNES

A book about the working-class program, composition, and course of the only kind of party in the imperialist epoch worthy of the name "revolutionary." A party that can recognize the most revolutionary fact of this epoch—the worth of working people, and our capacity to change society when we organize and act to win power from the capitalist class. $15. Also in Spanish, French, Farsi, Greek.

The Communist Manifesto

KARL MARX AND FREDERICK ENGELS

Communism, say the founding leaders of the revolutionary workers movement, is not a set of ideas or preconceived "principles" but workers' line of march to power. It springs from a "movement going on under our very eyes." $5. Also in Spanish, French, Farsi, Arabic.

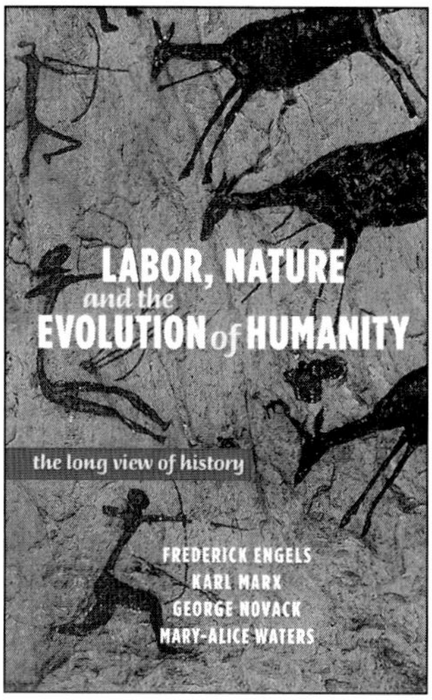

Labor, Nature, and the Evolution of Humanity

The Long View of History

FREDERICK ENGELS, KARL MARX
GEORGE NOVACK
MARY-ALICE WATERS

Without understanding that social labor, transforming nature, has driven humanity's evolution for millions of years, working people are unable to see beyond the capitalist epoch of class exploitation that warps all human relations, ideas, and values. $12. Also in Spanish and French.

In Defense of Marxism

Against the Petty-Bourgeois Opposition in the Socialist Workers Party

LEON TROTSKY

A reply to those in the revolutionary workers movement in the late 1930s who buckled to bourgeois patriotism during Washington's buildup to enter World War II. Trotsky explains why only a party fighting to bring workers into its ranks and leadership can steer a communist course. In the process, he defends the materialist and dialectical foundations of Marxism. $17. Also in Spanish, French, Farsi.

Tribunes of the People and the Trade Unions

KARL MARX, V.I. LENIN, LEON TROTSKY
FARRELL DOBBS, JACK BARNES

A tribune of the people uses every manifestation of capitalist oppression to explain why working people, in class battles, will break from the bosses' parties, organize a revolutionary fight for state power, and lay the foundations of a socialist world of human solidarity. $12. Also in Spanish, French, Farsi, Greek.

EXPAND YOUR REVOLUTIONARY LIBRARY

New Expanded Edition!

Cosmetics, Fashion, and the Exploitation of Women

MARY-ALICE WATERS
JOSEPH HANSEN, EVELYN REED

"Norms of beauty and fashion are inseparable from the class struggle." That's the title of the opening chapter of this timely new edition of a lively 1950s debate in the *Militant*, a socialist newsweekly. How cosmetics and fashion monopolies rake in profits from social insecurities of women and adolescents. Why women's integration into the workforce and unions is a major advance in the fight for emancipation. A Marxist classic on the origins of women's oppression and the working-class road forward. $15. Also in Spanish, French, Farsi, Greek.

Socialism on Trial

Testimony at Minneapolis Sedition Trial

JAMES P. CANNON

The revolutionary program of the working class presented in federal court in 1941 on the eve of US entry into World War II. The frame-up charges of "seditious conspiracy" targeted leaders of the Socialist Workers Party. $15. Also in Spanish, French, Farsi.

50 Years of Covert Operations in the US

Washington's Political Police and the American Working Class

LARRY SEIGLE, FARRELL DOBBS, STEVE CLARK

How class-conscious workers have defended constitutional freedoms and fought the capitalists' drive to build the "national security" state essential to maintaining their rule. $10. Also in Spanish and Farsi.

Lenin's Final Fight

Speeches and Writings, 1922–23

V.I. LENIN

In 1922 and 1923, V.I. Lenin, central leader of the world's first socialist revolution, waged what was to be his last political battle—one that was lost after his death. At stake was whether that revolutionary government and the world communist movement it led would remain on the revolutionary proletarian course that brought workers and peasants to power in Russia in 1917. $17. Also in Spanish, Farsi, Greek.

Malcolm X Talks to Young People

"The young generation of whites, Blacks, browns, whatever else—you're living at a time of revolution," said Malcolm in 1964. "And I for one will join with anyone, I don't care what color you are, as long as you want to change this miserable condition that exists on this earth." Four talks and an interview in the last months of Malcolm's life. $12. Also in Spanish, French, Farsi, Greek.

Pathfinder Press **accessible e-books** for the blind, those with low vision, or other challenges reading print books

For a list of current accessible titles, go to: pathfinderpress.com/collections/books-for-the-blind.

Visit bookshare.org for information on how to sign up.

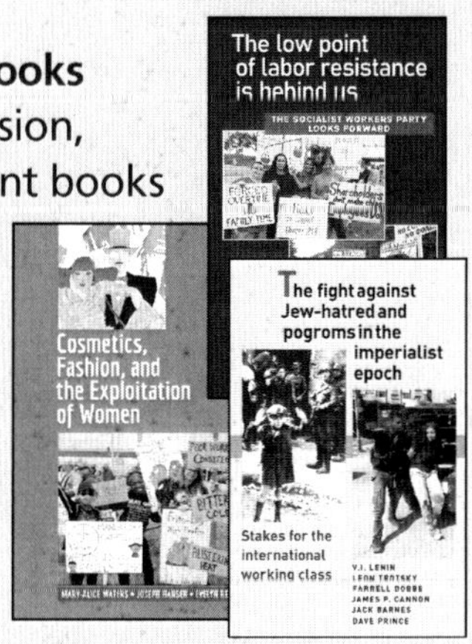